Goods and Services Tax (GST) in India

Goods and Services Tax (GST) in India

By

B. Viswanathan

Additional Director (Monitoring),
Special Programme Implementation Department,
Secretariat, Government of Tamil Nadu, Chennai

New Century Publications
New Delhi, India

NEW CENTURY PUBLICATIONS
4800/24, Bharat Ram Road,
Ansari Road, Daryaganj,
New Delhi - 110 002 (India)

Tel.: 011-2324 7798, 4358 7398, 6539 6605
Fax: 011-4101 7798
E-mail: indiatax@vsnl.com • info@newcenturypublications.com
www.newcenturypublications.com

Editorial office:
LG–7, Aakarshan Bhawan,
4754-57/23, Ansari Road, Daryaganj,
New Delhi – 110 002

Tel.: 011-4356 0919

First Published: **July 2016**

ISBN: **978-81-7708-429-0**

Published by New Century Publications and printed at Salasar Imaging Systems, New Delhi.

Designs: Patch Creative Unit, New Delhi.

PRINTED IN INDIA

Dedicated to the Great Souls

My Grandparents (Late) Shrimati and Shri B.K. Joghee Gowder

My Father (Late) Shri L. Bheema Gowder

My Nephew (Late) Master R. Manjit Raj

My Son (Late) Master Surya Viswanath

About the Book

Restructuring of the tax system has constituted a major component of fiscal reforms in India initiated since 1991. The main focus of the tax reforms has been on simplification and rationalization of both direct and indirect taxes with the objective of augmenting revenues and removing anomalies in the tax structure. Tax reforms in recent years have brought the tax system much closer to international tax practices.

In the 2016-17 Union Budget, gross tax revenue of the Government has been estimated at ₹ 16,30,888 crore. Out of this, the share of taxes on goods and services (customs, excise and service tax) is ₹ 7,83,791 crore (48.1 percent) while the remaining ₹ 8,47,097 crore (51.9 percent) is contributed by direct taxes (corporation tax and income tax).

The current structure of taxes on goods and services in India is highly complex, leaky (riddled with exemptions), and characterized by complicated compliance procedures. The strategy of the Government in respect of indirect taxes is to continue the tariff reforms process towards mean Asian levels of customs tariff, convergence towards a single rate of excise duty (with some exceptions), widening of service tax base and a phased move towards a fully-integrated goods and services tax (GST).

National level GST is a part of the proposed tax reforms to evolve an efficient and harmonized consumption tax system in the country. Presently, there are parallel systems of indirect taxes at the Central and State levels. Each of the systems needs to be reformed to eventually harmonize them.

This book traces the evolution of taxation of goods and services (indirect taxes) in India during the post-Independence period. More importantly, it analyzes the present structure of indirect taxes and the harmonization measures undertaken by the Government in this regard. It also examines and sets forth core issues pertaining to the proposed national level GST which is expected to be rolled out in the near future.

About the Author

Dr. B. Viswanathan is currently Additional Director (Monitoring) in the Special Programme Implementation Department, Secretariat, Government of Tamil Nadu, Chennai. He received his B.Sc. and M.Sc. degrees in Statistics from the Universities of Madras and Bharatiyar in 1983 and 1985 respectively. He obtained his M.A. (Economics) degree from Annamalai University in 1997 and Ph.D. (Economics) from Bharatiyar University in 2007.

Dr. Viswanathan joined the Tamil Nadu Statistical Service in 1994 as Assistant Director of Statistics. He has served in the Department of Commercial Taxes and State Planning Commission, Government of Tamil Nadu in various capacities. His areas of research interest include indirect taxes, Centre-State financial relations and planning.

Contents

Preface

Taxes are imposed so that a government may perform its traditional functions (defence, and maintenance of law and order), undertake welfare and developmental activities, and make provision for public goods to satisfy collective needs of the people. It has also to pay for its own administration. It needs financial resources for these purposes and taxation is one method of transferring money from private to public hands.

Restructuring of the tax system has constituted a major component of fiscal reforms initiated since 1991. The main focus of the tax reforms has been on simplification and rationalization of both direct and indirect taxes with the objective of augmenting revenues and removing anomalies in the tax structure. Tax reforms in recent years have brought the tax system much closer to international tax practices.

In the 2016-17 Union Budget, gross tax revenue of the Government has been estimated at ₹ 16,30,888 crore. Out of this, the share of taxes on goods and services (customs, excise and service tax) is ₹ 7,83,791 crore (48.1 percent) while the remaining ₹ 8,47,097 crore (51.9 percent) is contributed by direct taxes (corporation tax and income tax).

The current structure of taxes on goods and services in India is highly complex, leaky (riddled with exemptions), and characterized by complicated compliance procedures.

In relation to goods, the Centre has a very complex tax structure, more complex than that of most of the States. It encompasses customs, central excise, cesses, countervailing and special additional duties, extensive exemptions, and a multiplicity of rates (ad valorem and specific rates).

In relation to services too, the Centre has a complicated rate structure. Although there is one statutory rate, in practice there are 10 other rates because of the so-called *abatement* which amounts to fixing a rate different from the standard rate and not allowing further input tax credits. Abatement is necessitated in some part because of uncertainty in the base, and specifically being unable to distinguish *goods* from *services*. Further, there is incomplete provision of input tax crediting for goods, and incomplete cross-crediting between goods and services. Added to this is the Central sales tax (CST) which is levied on the sale or purchase of goods in the course of inter-State trade.

In relation to goods, the States have structures characterized by a base that is complete in extending all the way to the retail stage, an exemption threshold that varies across States, provision for *compounding* that also varies across States in design and a multiplicity of rates on inter-State trade (octroi, entry tax).

In short, indirect tax system of India is currently mired in multi-layered taxes levied by the Central and State Governments at different stages of the supply chain, viz. excise duty, value added tax (VAT), octroi and others.

The strategy of the Government in respect of indirect taxes is to continue the tariff reform process towards mean ASEAN levels of customs tariff, convergence towards CENVAT rate for excise duty, widening of service tax base and a phased move towards a fully integrated goods and services tax.

National level GST is a part of the proposed tax reforms to evolve an efficient and harmonized consumption tax system in the country. Presently, there are parallel systems of indirect taxation at the Central and State levels. Each of the system needs to be reformed to eventually harmonize them.

GST is proposed to be a comprehensive indirect tax levy on manufacture, sale and consumption of goods as well as services at the national level. GST would give India a world class tax system and improve tax collections. It would end the long standing distortions of differential treatment of manufacturing and service sector. The introduction of GST will lead to the abolition of various Central and State indirect taxes and eliminate the cascading effects of multiple layers of taxation. It is claimed that GST will facilitate seamless credit across the entire supply chain and across all states under a common tax base.

For nearly ten years, India has been on the verge of implementing the GST. But now, with political consensus close to being secured, the nation is on the verge of executing one of the most ambitious and remarkable tax reforms in its post-Independence history. Implementing a new tax, encompassing both goods and services, to be implemented by the Centre, 29 States and 2 Union Territories, in a large and complex federal system, via a Constitutional amendment requiring broad political consensus, is perhaps unprecedented in modern global tax history.

The Lok Sabha passed the 122nd Constitutional Amendment—Goods and Services Tax Bill on May 6, 2015. Currently, the hope is that GST will be implemented from April 1, 2017. Once the Parliament passes the GST Bill, 50 percent of the States will have to ratify it and then both the Centre and the States have to pass Central GST and State GST Bills respectively and rules have to be made under them. So far, the Government has failed to push the Constitutional amendment bill in the Rajya Sabha.

The changeover to GST will be a game-changing tax reform measure which will significantly contribute to the buoyancy of tax revenues, acceleration of growth, and generation of many positive externalities.

An attempt has been made in this book to trace the evolution of taxation of goods and services (indirect taxes) in India during the post-Independence period. More importantly, it analyzes the present structure of indirect taxes and the harmonization measures undertaken by the Government in this regard. It also examines and sets forth core issues pertaining to the proposed national level GST which is expected to be rolled out in the near future.

ACKNOWLEDGEMENTS

I take this opportunity to express my sincere thanks to Dr. K. Satyagopal (I.A.S.) Principal Secretary, Special Programme Implementation Department, Government of Tamil Nadu for accepting my request to publish this book. Also, I am indebted to my Director, Dr. K. Radhakrishnan, Special Programme Implementation Department, Government of Tamil Nadu for the encouragement, motivation and valuable suggestions.

I am grateful to my colleagues Mr. P. Selvaraj, Mr. S. Senthil Kumar, Mr. P. Gopal, Mr. G. Thiagarajan, Mrs. Revathy and other friends who helped me at various stages of the preparation of this book.

Finally, I place on record my deep appreciation for my wife Mrs. Sugumari Viswanathan and my daughter Miss Sandhya Viswanathan who both provided the moral support and conducive atmosphere to complete this arduous task.

Chennai **B. Viswanathan**

1

Goods and Services Tax (GST) in India: Recent Reforms

1.1 Central Level Reforms (MODVAT/CENVAT)

Fiscal reforms in India have been carried out from time to time and these reform measures were initially aimed at mobilization of resources to meet the exigencies of plan targets. Later, the focus was on the rationalization, simplification and harmonization of taxes and tariff structures.

The Indirect Taxation Enquiry Committee (1978) laid the basic foundation for the introduction of value added tax at the manufacturing level (MODVAT, and later CENVAT) in India to mitigate primarily the influence of cascading input taxes by permitting credits for the taxes paid on inputs and harmonization of innumerable tax rates to a reasonable number.

Further, the Tax Reforms Committee (TRC) 1991, headed by the country's senior fiscal expert, Professor Raja Chelliah, did the most pioneering study for restructuring and rationalization of tax system in India.

The TRC brought forward three reports: (a) An interim report in December 1991, (b) final report Part I in August 1992 and (c) final report Part II in January 1993 and these reports formed the basis for the Union government to carry out its reform agenda on simplification, rationalization and harmonization.

India's domestic trade reforms have been initiated following a study done by the National Institute of Public Finance and Policy (NIPFP) in 1994 to examine the various designs for a coordinated consumption tax system in India.

The report titled "Reform of Domestic Trade Taxes in India" recommended a dual VAT: a central VAT to be levied by the Central Government by converting the union excise duty into CENVAT at the manufacturing level and a state VAT to be adopted by the state Governments by replacing the existing sales tax into a full-fledged VAT at the wholesale and the subsequent retail level to maintain a balance between sub-national fiscal autonomy and the ability of the Centre to undertake any desired interstate redistribution.

Subsequently, the Task Force on Indirect Taxes (2002) under the chairmanship of Dr. Vijay Kelkar, advisor to the Ministry of Finance and Company Affairs, recommended further rationalization of tax structure, such as reduction of multiple levies of excise system into a single levy of CENVAT, lowering of exemption ceiling, abolition of multiple schemes for export promotion and encouragement of export promotion through special economic zones (SEZs) and export-oriented units (EOUs).

Towards tax harmonization and revenue mobilisation, the Fiscal Responsibility and Budget Management Act, 2003 recommended various suggestions to convert the CENVAT into a genuine VAT at the central level, improve the tax-GDP ratio by integrating goods and services in CENVAT, converse tax base from production to consumption designed on the destination principle and avail credits for all the intermediate goods and services, so as to mitigate the influence of cascading of input taxes and reduction of threshold level for the small-scale sector.

1.1.1 Modified Value Added Tax (MODVAT): Introduction of MODVAT in 1986 was the first and foremost reform measure undertaken in the Independent India based on the recommendations of the Indirect Taxation Enquiry Committee under the Chairmanship of L.K. Jha.

The MODVAT system permits the manufacturers to obtain instant and complete reimbursement of excise duty paid on components and raw materials.

It was intended to mitigate cascading input taxation, rationalization of tax rates and simplification of tax procedures to improve the efficiency and tax compliance. During 2000-01, the MODVAT scheme was renamed as CENVAT with a single tax rate of 16 percent.

A study conducted by the National Institute of Public Finance and Policy on "Operation of MODVAT" shows that MODVAT scheme seems to have had a mitigating influence on the cascading effect of multistage excise taxation.

The coverage of commodities under MODVAT was incremental and not comprehensive as certain sectors such as oil and gas production, agriculture, wholesale and retail trade and construction remain outside the scope of CENVAT.

These sectors cannot claim any ITC under CENVAT and service tax. Moreover, many commodities were exempted from CENVAT and the tax rate also reduced for selected commodities.

The Central Sales Tax (CST) levied on interstate trade is the most contributing factor to tax cascading as the tax is collected by the exporting state for which no ITC is permitted.

Tax cascading is huge under CENVAT, service tax and State VAT due to the innumerable exemptions and restricted ITC claims. Also, exclusion of services from both CENVAT and State VAT and the failure of the Central Government to extend taxation beyond manufacturing and trade reduce the assessable value of goods artificially low and create confusion as to what constitutes the "sale of goods".

Hence, during contingencies, states resorted to setting tax rates beyond the floor rates.

1.2 State Level Value Added Tax (VAT)

Tax harmonization is very essential to make the goods and services globally competitive and on these lines, most of the countries, worldwide, have formed common trading blocks known as regional blocks in order to reap the benefits under large common markets by exploiting the economies of scale.

Creation of such common markets become significant for a federal country like India as it improves the efficiency of internal economies, productivity of factors resulting in higher growth rates, reduction of consumer price dispersion and enhancement of employment prosperity for citizens.

Among the various barriers for the free flow of goods, services, capital and labour such as physical and technical; fiscal barriers act as a stumbling block for the creation of common market, as they cause distortions in consumption, production and externalities, thereby impairing the growth of federal economies.

Among the various taxes, indirect taxes are closely associated with the distortions and externalities in production as well as in consumption.

Hence, there is a need to harmonize domestic trade taxes viz. central excise, sales tax/VAT and service tax and the efforts towards such harmonization, which have been hailed as the greatest fiscal innovation of the 20th century.

At the state level, replacing the sales tax system with VAT is regarded as the *boldest tax reform undertaken in Independent India.* The half a century old sales taxes levied by the States was so complex and the VAT has mitigated this complex structure in taxation to a certain extent.

The first point sales taxation with its multiple forms such as surcharges, turnover tax and additional sales tax, etc., has distorted the indirect taxation in India and the multiplicity of tax rates often lead to confusion in drawing distinctions among goods that were often flawed and led to endless disputes.

On January 17, 2005, a White Paper released by the Empowered Committee outlined the basic structure of State VAT.

1.2.1 Features of Uniform State Level VAT: Some of the important features of a uniform State VAT, as brought out by the White Paper, are given below:

1. There will be uniform tax rates of 4 percent and 12.5 percent in addition to 1 percent in case of precious stones and precious metals and an exemption of 46 items.
2. VAT credits are allowed for all taxes paid on purchases within the States from the VAT payable by a dealer and cover all raw materials, capital goods and items purchased

for resale by the registered dealers. Exports and sale to special economic zones would be zero-rated.

3. VAT credit will be available on purchase of input materials and capital goods.
4. No credit will be allowed for taxes paid on purchases made outside a particular State.
5. States can continue with the existing sales tax incentives committed earlier, without breaking the VAT chain.
6. The opening stocks as on April 1, 2005 would be eligible for input tax credit, provided such purchases are made within a period of one year prior to this date, i.e., after March 31, 2004.

The feature of VAT uniformity agreed by the States is a major step in the direction of reforming state taxes and is considered as a major step towards harmonization of State sales tax system.

Even though most of the States implemented VAT since April 2005, the implementation of VAT in States has its own problems.

Exclusion of services, continuation of exemptions and concessions, no credit for inputs purchased outside the State and variation in fixing threshold limits are some of the demerits in the operation of VAT in States.

One of the major shortcomings is the non-application of floor rates in some States where some items have been brought down from 12.5 percent to 4 percent and some commodities from 4 percent to 0 percent, resulted in wide variation and the very purpose of setting floor rates has been defeated.

This diversion of trade goes against the principle of tax harmonization. The application of VAT on MRP (maximum retail price) at the first point on drugs in West Bengal and Maharashtra goes against the principle of VAT, as there would be no addition of value at the subsequent stages.

The wide variation of 8.5 percent between the tax rates of inputs and outputs (4 percent and 12.5 percent) may result in revenue loss to the government, as many commodities are used as inputs as well as outputs and the manufacturers are enticed to suppress the sale of outputs and prefer to pay 4 percent on inputs. The wide variation towards the tax rates of inputs and outputs may encourage lobbying to cover more number of commodities in future. In fact, no country in the world, where VAT is operated, offers concessional treatment of inputs.

According to the report of the Comptroller and Auditor General of India (CAG), ten States have registered a fall in the average growth of revenue during the post-VAT regime against those relating to the pre-VAT periods.

These included few of the major States like Gujarat and Tamil Nadu. Further, the Report also pointed out that in spite of a quantum increase in tax base in all the States after implementation of VAT, the deceleration can mainly be attributed to tax evasion.

1.3 Introduction and Evolution of Service Tax

Starting with a mere three services in 1994, service tax has been extended to almost all services over the years and instantaneously the tax rate has also increased from 5 percent to 14 percent. Among the various services, trade, hotels and restaurants, communication, business services, financial services and community services have exhibited phenomenal growth during the post-reforms period.

Under the business services, information technology (IT) sector grew at an annual rate of more than 25 percent and NASSCOM (National Association of Software and Service Companies), an apex body of IT and ITES in India, has predicted an extraordinary growth in future.

Retail industry too holds huge potential and opportunities for growth of revenue from the service sector. As service tax is going to be a major source of revenue in the future, a harmonized tax system covering goods, services and trade would play a pivotal role in the indirect tax system in future.

Hence, at the manufacturing level, service tax should be integrated with the CENVAT and at the State level it should be integrated with the State VAT, in order to have a harmonized tax system. A Constitutional amendment is also necessary to empower the States to tax services to augment the revenue of the States.

1.4 National Level Goods and Services Tax (GST)

To overcome the deficiencies in CENVAT and State VAT dispensations, the Union Finance Minister while presenting the Union Budget proposals for the fiscal year 2006-07, had announced that the government would introduce Goods and Services Tax from April 1, 2010.

Subsequently, the present Union Finance Minister Mr. Arun Jaitley also hailed the introduction of Goods and Services Tax from April 2016 as the biggest tax reform since Independence.

The Constitution Amendment Bill, 2014, was introduced, which sought to amend the Constitution to introduce the goods and services tax (GST).

Consequently, the GST would subsume various central indirect taxes including the central excise duty, countervailing duty, service tax, etc. It will also subsume State value added tax, octroi and entry tax, luxury tax etc.

The Bill provides concurrent powers to both the Central and State governments to make laws on the taxation of goods and services.

An Integrated GST (IGST) is to be levied only by the Centre on supplies in the course of inter-state trade or commerce. The tax collected would be divided between the Centre and the States in a manner to be provided by the Parliament and by law, on the recommendations of the GST Council.

The GST Council consists of the following three members: (i) the Union Finance Minister (as chairman), (ii) the Union Minister of State in-charge of revenue or finance, and (iii) the Minister in-charge of finance or taxation or any other, nominated by each State Government.

The functions of the GST Council include making

recommendations on the following:

1. Taxes, cesses, and surcharges levied by the Centre, States and local bodies which may be subsumed in the GST.
2. Goods and services which may be subjected to or exempted from GST.
3. Model GST laws, principles of levy, apportionment of IGST and principles that govern the place of supply.
4. Threshold limit of turnover below which goods and services may be exempted from GST.
5. Rates including floor rates, with bands of GST.
6. Special rates to raise additional resources during any natural calamity.
7. Special provision with respect to Arunachal Pradesh, Jammu and Kashmir, Manipur, Meghalaya, Mizoram, Nagaland, Sikkim, Tripura, Himachal Pradesh and Uttarakhand.
8. Deciding the modalities for the resolution of disputes arising out of its recommendations.

The States will be paid compensation up to a five year period for revenue losses on account of the implementation of the GST. Alcoholic liquor is exempted and the GST Council has to decide on the levy to be imposed on petroleum crude, high speed diesel, motor spirit, natural gas, and aviation turbine fuel. For consumers, GST will reduce prices of goods and services and in the long run there will be convergence of prices across the country, which would enhance the overall growth of the economy.

In his Budget Speech to the Parliament on June 10, 2014, the Finance Minister made the following observations regarding GST, "The debate whether to introduce a Goods and Services Tax (GST) must now come to an end. We have discussed the issue for the past many years. Some States have been apprehensive about surrendering their taxation jurisdiction; others want to be adequately compensated. I have discussed the matter with the States both individually and collectively. I do hope we are able to find a solution in the course of this year and approve the legislative scheme which enables the introduction of GST. This will streamline the tax administration, avoid harassment of the business and result in higher revenue collection both for the Centre and the States. I assure all States that government will be more than fair in dealing with them". [1]

In his Budget Speech to the Parliament on February 28, 2015, the Finance Minister observed on GST as follows, "We need to revive growth and investment to ensure that more jobs are created for our youth and benefits of development reach millions of our poor. We need an enabling tax policy for this. I have already introduced the Bill to amend the Constitution of India for Goods and Services Tax (GST) in the last Session of this august House. GST is expected to play a transformative role in the way our economy functions. It will add buoyancy to our economy by developing a common Indian market and reducing the cascading effect on the cost of goods and services. We are moving in various fronts to implement GST from the next year". [2]

Endnotes

1. Government of India, Ministry of Finance, *Budget Speech of the Finance Minister, 2014-15.*
2. Government of India, Ministry of Finance, *Budget Speech of the Finance Minister, 2015-16,* para *96.*

2

Tax Harmonization and Creation of Common Market in a Federal Polity

2.1 Tax Harmonization Defined

Harmonization of tax is defined as the "process of removing the fiscal barriers and differences between the tax systems of various countries within a trade block or between sub-national governments in a federation". In this definition, the removal of fiscal barriers means the goods and services imported receives the same treatment as the domestically manufactured products and the removal of differences between the tax systems refers to bringing tax systems into harmony or agreement.

Dosser (1973), states that tax harmonization is the "tax co-ordination among nations in the process of integration in a customs union or economic union". But this definition is not sufficient in describing the current usage of the term. Prest (1979) describes co-ordination as a consultation process for organising tax system in a similar way. But, Rounds (1992) refers harmonization as any situation where difference in taxation between member states in a federation is reduced either by co-operation or by a federal policy. Musgrave (1967) views harmonization as a process of adjusting national fiscal systems to conform to a set of common economic aims.

Under the European Community context, harmonization means "the process of planning, which aims to approximate tax systems of different member states in order to achieve the common objectives of the community".

Mintz and Wilson (1991) opined, "any degree of co-ordination leading to an improvement in the alternative administration and equality impacts of a tax system in a federation"—this definition refers harmonization as a mechanism to reduce the spillover effects between the jurisdictions caused by the reckless tax competition among the constituent units against federal welfare.

According to Cnossen, tax coordination is "any change in the tax system with the aim of creating an integrated market free of restrictions on the movement of goods, the abolition of obstacles to the right of establishment of businesses and employment and to the free movement of persons, services and capital and the institution of a system ensuring that competition is not distorted". As set out by Cnossen, harmonization requires not only the abolition of fiscal barriers but also the co-ordination of major indirect taxes and some direct taxes to improve the smooth functioning of a common market.

Mitchell (2004) states that tax harmonization exist when tax payers face similar or identical tax rates no matter where they work, save, shop, or invest. Harmonized tax rates eliminate fiscal competition—such as, a floor price-fixing agreement between states on selected commodities. Tax harmonization can be achieved by two different ways such as explicit tax harmonization which occurs when jurisdictions agree to set minimum tax rates or decide to tax at the same rate. In the case of European Union, it requires that member nations impose a value added tax (VAT) of at least 15 percent. Implicit harmonization occurs when governments tax the income of their citizens who earn in other jurisdictions. This requires governments to collect financial information on non-resident investors and to share that information with tax collecting agencies in foreign governments.

The term tax harmonization has a plethora of meanings. Commonly, it signifies the following alternate close definitions.

- **Tax Convergence**: Due to competitive pressure, bringing tax systems and tax rates among the member states closer.
- **Tax Approximation:** Due to political agreements between member states, bringing tax systems and tax rates closer without becoming identical.

- **Tax Co-ordination:** Making similar tax practices among member states by means of non-legislative measures like conventions, guidelines etc.

2.2 Types of Harmonization

Harmonization takes different forms depending on the degree of tax harmonization possible in a decentralized federal tax system.

2.2.1 Strong Harmonization: In this form, the federal government, in consultation with the different levels of governments, collects taxes assigned to different levels and the total taxes collected are shared among the constitutional units according to a pre-agreed formula between the federal and its constituent units. In this form, the states are passive recipients of revenue collected by the federal government, but a uniform tax system is achieved with equity and efficiency at a lower cost.

2.2.2 Similar Form Harmonization: In this form, as in the case of strong harmonization, the advantage of the central collecting authority is retained while some revenue raising responsibility is assigned to the states. The federal government determines both the base and the rate structure and the states are empowered to set a state tax rate on the same base that would determine the proportion of revenue owed to the state. The Central (Federal) authority collects the tax on behalf of the states and passes it on to the states.

2.2.3 Weak Harmonization: Harmonization is said to be weak if tax credits are allowed at one level of government while determining the tax payable to others such as deducting the state sales taxes while determining the tax base of corporate income tax levied by the federal government. Weak harmonization is said to be in the extreme form where the federal government decides the tax base, tax rate, collects the revenue and share the proceeds with the constituent units—such as the union excise duty and income tax in India.

Commencing with no harmonization, the first step towards

harmonization would be administrative co-operation between personnel of taxes of different jurisdictions on the tax bases falling within or more than one jurisdiction. The next stage would be to avoid double taxation through agreements so as to avoid the same tax base so that it is not taxed twice. The next stage would be the examination of some of the taxes that would lead to a partial harmonization. The next important stage towards full form of harmonization would be levying same taxes with different tax bases and approaches in the administration of taxes called the "nominal harmonization". Finally, the extreme or the strong form of harmonization would be to have same taxes with the same tax bases and same tax rates known as the complete standardization of harmonization.

2.3 Federal Polity and Creation of Common Markets

Federations are commonly characterized as a union or association of two or more federating units having different ethnic backgrounds, language, culture, etc. At the topmost level, there is a federal (central) government and at lower levels (state and municipal) there are governments each having a well-defined set of functions and resources to discharge their duties efficiently. Alexis de Tocqueville suggests that "the federal system was developed with the intention of aggregating the different advantages which result from the magnitude and littleness of nations". [1] Taxation under multilevel governments largely depends on the suitability of taxes at each level of government, commonly referred to as "tax assignment problems". These federal economies over a long period evolved mechanisms through which they determined the allocation of tax bases among the various levels of government and allocate funds from one level to another. These federations draw political and economic strength from its federating units.

Under globalization of economies, economics has taken precedence over politics and there is a strong recognition of economic development of countries and international competitiveness of their economies. In this scenario, most countries world over have initiated several reform processes aimed at higher growth rates by exploiting the economies of scale, possible under the large common markets. Hence, many countries recognize the economic benefits they can reap under large common markets where the market forces are allowed to play a vital role in determining the allocation of resources, the location of industries and the factors of production under the conditions of competition. Such countries have formed common trading blocks, commonly known as "regional economic integration" such as the European Economic Union, North American Free Trade Agreement (NAFTA), South Asian Free Trade Area (SAFTA), Organisation for Economic Cooperation and Development (OECD), etc.

The concept of economic integration implies the process of abolishing some impediments that discriminate foreign goods, services, capital and labour. Complete integration denotes the removal of all barriers to free movement of goods, services, capital and labour. Economic integration is vital as it improves the productivity of factors resulting in the increase of real income. Further, it equalizes the prices of like products and factors and of income levels within the region. Empirical studies undertaken have demonstrated that integrated economies have a positive impact on the growth rate over time. It is said that integrated economies establish single markets.

The notion of single market originates from the European Union where the Treaty of Rome created in 1957 was a common market. The European Common Market is based on the free movement of goods, services, capital and labour. The single market is something more than the common market. The single European Act defines single market as an area without internal frontiers in which free movement of goods, persons, services and capital is ensured. The main idea behind the single market is that there should not be any discrimination in any of the regional markets for goods, services or factors without geographical segmentation.

Small-segmented markets are unable to manufacture goods profitably with increasing returns to scale through declining production costs. Scale economies in such segmented markets imply a few manufacturers who can sustain and survive with monopoly power resulting in high prices, low scales and higher costs. But in large unified single markets, manufacturers are subject to increased competition, leading to reduced prices and expansion of sales benefiting consumers due to the fall in monopolistic tendencies. The major gain in large single markets is the achievement of economies of scale due to the availability of huge market size. In segmented markets, given the market size, the trade-off between scale economies and competition makes a few firms to survive and the market becomes less competitive.

However, in large single markets, this trade-off fails and there would be more firms and greater competition. This intense competition leads to merger or closure of some firms resulting in a few efficient ones. The overall effect would be the intense competition, enhanced firm scale and reduced costs. Ultimately, larger and efficient firms can better exploit economies of scale. Further, intense competition increases the chance of mergers and closures and it induces the firms and the workers to remove the internal inefficiencies and improve productivity.

Economists have defined single market as one in which the law of one price must hold in goods, services, and factor markets. This implies that there should be a single price for each tradable commodity and factors in the entire market area where all prices are expressed in single currency and adjusting for the real costs of moving goods or factors between locations. Hence, the single market integrates the entire market area completely by permitting the real costs of moving goods or factors from one area to another. Single markets require perfect competition as against imperfect competition where markets are segmented by having different prices in different segments of the market, which will not equalize prices across the segments. Further, it requires the dissemination information on goods and services. Full information will lead to arbitrage that will establish a single price within the nation, adjusting for the costs of transport between different places within the market area.

A single market is significant for federations as it suppresses all discrimination in goods and factor markets against goods and factors produced by suppliers in different sub-national governments. Under the standard general equilibrium theory, establishment of single market or the abolition of border or non-border controls is a precondition for Pareto-efficient production and distribution allocations. The creation of single market will improve the efficiency of sub-national economies in a federation or countries within a trade block by permitting them to specialize in the production of goods in which they have a comparative advantage.

Free movement of labour will further increase the output by shifting to locations where marginal productivity is the greatest. Similarly, free movement of capital improves an efficient allocation of savings and puts resources into their most productive uses. Creation of single market increases the level of competition among the different producers and this intense competition reduces the cost and prices and improves product diversity. Building single markets have a positive impact on prices, as it tends to reduce the price variation for like products. Other way round, it reduces the price dispersion for all markets, those of the goods and services and for factors as well as product markets.

Creation of single markets improves the convergence of incomes. Convergence of income means, the lessening of measures of inequality among the different jurisdictions/countries in a federation/trade block. Empirical studies have proved that substantial convergence of incomes is possible between the different jurisdictions. Poorer jurisdictions/countries in a federation/trade block significantly grew faster than the rich countries, leading to a sharp decline in the inter-jurisdiction income inequality. Apart from the convergence of prices and incomes, single markets quicken the rate of growth of real GDP and converge mean incomes of individual economies. Empirical studies show a consistent positive correlation between higher growth rates and higher level of trade due to the single market.

A study funded by the European Commission in 1988, called Cecchini Report, concluded that under the single European market, there was a 4.5 percent increase in European Union GDP with low inflation and projected that if all countries under European Union (EU) take appropriate actions, there would be a 7.5 percent growth in European Union generating 5.7 million new jobs. [2] Later in 2002, a similar study conducted by the European Commission suggested that since 1992, the single market boosted the EU GDP by 1.8 percentage points, enhanced household income by 6,000 euros per household, increased foreign direct investment by 12 times, increased exports to 11.2 percent in 2002 and created 2.5 million jobs.

The subject of single market incorporates the removal of all impediments to trade within a federation/economic block in order to unify the sub-national/country markets into single markets by making conditions close to the genuine internal market. The economic benefits of single markets "serves as a driving force in economic integration in a way that the resources would be made more productive with increases in consumption and investment through cost reductions resulting from the exploitation of economies to scale, increased competition, leading to enhanced economic efficiency, cost reduction arising from industrial restructuring to exploit comparable advantage of member states and flow of innovations, new processes and products, stimulated by a single market". [3] It is believed that the development of a single market would lead to an acceleration of economic growth and hence to increased prosperity for the citizens.

The development of single market involves the elimination

of all obstacles within a trading block or federation for the free movement of goods, persons, services and capital. But there are three types of barriers including physical, technical and fiscal. Only upon removal of these barriers, the achievement of a single market is possible.

2.4 Physical Barriers

These are the interstate border check posts in a federation or the customs posts, immigration controls and the passport verification centres which exist along the borders between countries in a trade block. These controls are maintained to collect tax, trade statistics and for enforcement of regulations for controlling the movement of goods and labour. Such interstate physical barriers impede the free flow of goods and services within a single market. These physical controls can be removed by abolishing the check posts and the immigration controls without sacrificing the accuracy of statistical information on trade. Abolition of border controls alone does not suffice the creation of a genuine common market. But it is the free movement of people, goods and companies within a trade block. These barriers impede trade flows, causing distortions in production patterns, adding administrative costs and increasing the stockholding costs and frustrating the development of common markets. As a result, traders pay more attention to the exploitation of the local markets rather than markets within the trade block and find it difficult to benefit from the economies of scale of a genuine unified market.

2.5 Technical Barriers

These include different national product standards, different technical regulations and qualifications and divergent business laws. These barriers hinder the mobility of labour and capital. The regulations that exist in one state may not be recognized elsewhere and the movement of capital is hindered by the legislation governing the financial markets and exchange transactions. Establishing equivalent qualifications where the degrees and diplomas awarded in one state should be recognized in other states/countries within a federation/ trade block pave the way for the free mobility of labour. Adopting uniform rules for streamlining the services such as deregulation of insurance, banking and finance and developing an integrated securities market linking all stock exchanges, the deregulation of modes of transport and abolishing exchange controls, will remove the barrier to the free mobility of capital.

2.6 Fiscal Barriers

These are the different type of taxes and tax systems prevalent in different jurisdictions in a federation. In a federal polity, public goods and services of national importance such as defence, money supply, international relations, etc., are assigned to the federal government whereas certain public goods such as water supply, health services and education are assigned to the local government. The assignment of taxes to provide the given public services in different jurisdictions with different tax capacities leaves the lower levels of government to levy different tax rates to their citizens.

In such circumstances, people in different states or countries paying different rates of tax for the same service depends on the state in which they reside. In fact, each sub-national government in a federation enjoys independent fiscal powers along with the functions that can be performed efficiently. These tax differentials and the different systems of taxation between the different levels of government distort trade and free mobility of factor flows, resulting in an inefficient allocation and if a sub-national government is well endowed with physical resources and manufacturing industries, taxes can also be exported to others depending on the relative competitive strength of their products.

In both the cases, efficiency and equity suffer as the former causes distortions in efficient allocation of production and consumption and the latter results in the encroachment of tax base of one jurisdiction by another and ultimately impairing the growth of the federal economy. Hence, there is a need for tax harmonization and co-ordination among the lower levels of government in a federation. Generally, in federations, the central (federal) governments have *enormous fiscal powers* to perform their functions. This calls for harmonization between the federal and sub-national taxes that is termed vertical harmonization. At the same time, federal government has to bear the problems arising from the allocation of tax powers at the different levels of government. This leads to the need for horizontal harmonization.

Under the globalization scenario, sustainability of higher taxes rates is very difficult as the economic integration under globalization knits separate economies into a single unified free market as a result of higher trade and investment flows, larger mobility of labour and increased technology transfers. Hence, in recent years, many countries around the world have implemented tax reforms to make their economies attractive for investment. For instance in Ireland, that has a population of 3.8 million people, the corporate tax has been reduced to just 10 percent on manufacturing and financial services which has attracted more foreign direct services and investment as compared to other countries. As a consequence, its economy spurred growth and now has one of the highest standards of living in the world. [4]

Tax harmonization contributes to the efficiency of internal single market, reduce collection and compliance costs and help achieve national standards of equity which can be achieved without sacrificing the state fiscal responsibility by having a single centralized collection procedure combined with meaningful powers of the states to decide on their own tax rates. [5]

The combined effect of physical, technical and fiscal barriers put a huge burden on all economic agents such as producers, consumers and business firms. The additional cost incurred by companies engaged in cross-border transactions often discourages cross border trade resulting in market fragmentation. Depending on the size of the trade agents, individuals and SMEs (small and medium entrepreneurs) stand to loose most from the fragmented market as they have to bear a substantial cost in cross border deals. The presence of fragmented markets impair the competitiveness of large common markets under federal countries in terms of its capacity to reap the benefits of economies of scale to compete with large integrated markets of United States and Japan.

Among these three barriers, fiscal barriers are more serious than the other two in federal countries as physical and technical barriers may be removed through legislative measures. Under fiscal barriers, unilateral measures by the federal governments would be met with stiff political ramifications such as loss of fiscal autonomy, etc. The removable of these barriers form the basis for the formation of a common market. In order to remove fiscal barriers, tax harmonization is highly essential in federations. Hence, it becomes necessary to discuss the rationale behind tax harmonization.

2.7 Rationale

Tax differentials across the jurisdictions in a federation causes two types of distortions namely, consumption and production.

2.7.1 Consumption Distortion: When a sub-national government in a federation levies on goods and services consumed within its borders, irrespective of whether the goods and services are produced within its borders or not, the taxation principle underlying is said to be the destination principle. Under this principle, uniform rate of tax applies to imports as well as domestically produced products whereas the exports are exempted from tax. If t_1 is the tax rate levied and P1 be the producer price, then the consumer prices will be $P_1 + t_1$. As free trade implies equalization of after tax prices, producer prices will be equalized across the sub-national governments, leading to an efficient production.

As an example, consider two sub-national governments, G_1 and G_2 and P_1 and P_2 to be the producer prices respectively on an identical commodity that follows destination principle and by levying imports at the same rate (t_1,t_2), the after price equalisation conditions for a commodity produced at home and imported will be:

$(P_1+t_1) = (P_1+t_2)$ home state (1)

$(P_2+t_1)= (P_2+t_2)$ foreign state (2)

which means $P_1=P_2$, i.e., as the producers equalizing this price to the rate of transformation between any two tradable goods, this rate will be the same in all the sub-national jurisdictions and the production efficiency is attained. On the consumption side, the consumers are indifferent across the jurisdictions on purchasing a locally made good and its import substitute. Hence, a *cross country fiscal neutrality* is achieved. On the other hand, if tax rates differ across jurisdictions, the consumer prices between identical tradable goods is not equalised across jurisdictions and the allocation of consumption becomes inefficient ultimately leading to consumption distortion.

2.7.2 Production Distortion: When a sub-national government levies taxes on all goods and services and produces within its borders, irrespective of the final consumption, the taxation principle is said to be the origin. Therefore, the exports are taxed and the imports are exempted. If t_1 and t_2 are the rate of taxes applied to goods produced at two sub-national governments, consumer prices will be:

$(P+t_1) = (P + t_2)$ (3)

which means $t_1=t_2$, i.e., the consumers are equating the relative consumer prices to the marginal rate of substitution. If the marginal rate of substitution is equated across countries, there is an efficient allocation of consumption. Hence, the origin principle ensures that producers are indifferent across the jurisdictions whereas the destination principle ensures that consumers are indifferent across jurisdictions. On the other hand, if tax rates differ across jurisdictions, the producer prices differ and there is an inefficient production leading to production distortion.

A. Under the Destination Principle:

- From the consumer point, neutrality is achieved, as the consumers are indifferent on purchasing a product whether it is produced internally or imported.
- Efficiency of production is achieved, as the marginal rates of transformation are the same across jurisdictions.
- Inefficiency in consumption if marginal rates of substitution differs across jurisdictions.

B. Under the Origin Principle:

- From the producer point, neutrality is achieved, as the producers are indifferent across the markets whether internal or external.
- Efficiency in consumption is achieved as the marginal rate of substitution is equalised across jurisdictions.
- Inefficiency in production as the marginal rate of transformation differs across jurisdictions.

From the above results, attainment of neutrality is based on the assumption that consumers are not crossing the border to buy goods where after tax price is lower as well as the producers are not moving their industries to a jurisdiction where after tax price is higher. If the assumption fails, neutrality achieved both under origin and destination also fails as the economic decisions are disturbed by the tax differentials across the jurisdictions. Hence, in evolving the tax policies, it is necessary to decide whether the tax policy strives for production efficiency or consumption efficiency or for a compromise between the two. According to the famous "Production Efficiency Theorem" of Diamond and Mirreless (1971), in a competitive economy, a Pareto-efficient tax structure is characterized by production efficiency and there are no restrictions on the distorting tax instruments and the taxation system is tilted in favour of the destination principle. [6]

In general, it is considered that moving industries from one jurisdiction to another is more important than cross border movement of consumers. Hence, under the destination principle, neutrality is *achieved in consumption while at the same time, ensuring efficient production.* Hence, destination principle generally is more preferred than the origin principle and it is unlikely to distort the location of economic activity or to result in tax competition between jurisdictions of residence. [7] By adopting uniform tax rates across the jurisdictions and by preventing inefficiencies in production and consumption and cross border movements, tax harmonization can be achieved irrespective of the taxation principle leading to the neutrality of tax systems.

2.8 Externalities or the Cross Border Taxation

Abolishing border controls without equalisation of taxes poses problems as the people in the border areas move out of borders to purchase commodities where taxes are low. As a result, jurisdictions having higher tax rate are found to loose a part of the revenue, causing negative impact on revenue (externality). This negative externality puts the jurisdictions to engage in tax competition.

Mintz and Tulkens (1986), [8] did a pioneering study on the implications of cross border shopping between the states in federations. The magnitude of cross border shopping is directly associated with the transportation costs and the difference in tax rates. If the difference between tax rates is small, then cross border shopping will be less attractive. On the other hand, if the tax difference is more, it will attract more people from the high tax jurisdictions to engage in cross border shopping in low tax jurisdictions. In between these two extremes, a substantial cross border shopping occurs between the states in federations that would largely depend on two types of tax externalities, namely a private consumption effect (negative) and a public consumption effect (positive).

A public consumption effect occurs as a result of the increased tax revenues (in the low taxed state), which can be used to improve the level of public goods. A private consumption effect occurs as a result of the loss of real income due to the increase in tax rates by the neighbouring state. The most likely impact of these two effects is directly related to the preference of the states facing the policy choices in regard to private and public consumption. De Crombrugghe and Tulkens (1990), proved that unhealthy commodity tax competition between states in federations always leads to setting of lower taxes in all the jurisdictions in spite of the counteracting private and public consumption effects in the higher tax states. Further, Keen and Kotsogiannis (2002), stated that "intensified tax competition within federal states worsens inefficiencies, ignoring the vertical externalities existing in federal systems". [9]

In open border scenarios with harmful tax competition between the states, a significant population residing near the border areas prefers to engage in cross border shopping, leading to the loss of revenues for the bigger jurisdictions and the smaller jurisdictions lose their ability to extract surplus from its citizens and revenue gains, provided the tax differentials are significantly great. [10] Small jurisdictions levy taxes at lower levels to attract more consumers from large jurisdictions to compensate for the low tax rate, leading to higher revenues. This externality disturbs the setting of a tax rate for ensuring the stability of revenues across the jurisdictions. Similarly, jurisdictions having market power, export tax burden to others by taxing imports and exports resulting in lower prices for producers in other jurisdictions and higher prices for its own consumers.

Under the destination principle, if a jurisdiction taxes imports more than exports, the consumer price of the imports increases with a fall in demand and vice versa for exports, resulting in the improvement of trade with respect to producer prices. Under the origin principle, if a jurisdiction taxes exports more than imports, the imports will replace exports with an excess demand for exports and the consumer price of exports will lead to an improvement of trade with respect to consumer prices. The impact of these distortions and externalities leads to substantial loss in terms of welfare and equity. [11]

2.9 Significance of Tax Harmonization

2.9.1 Revenue Stabilization and Evasion: Rash competition of tax rates among the jurisdictions in a federation or in a trading block, in order to attract investments from other jurisdictions, leads to reduction in tax revenues and in the long run, will cause unemployment with reduced public services. As the jurisdictions in a federation compete with others to attract investment, they reduce trade taxes. But they have to increase other taxes such as personal income tax or corporate taxes to compensate for the loss due to the lowering of trade taxes, leading to loss of employment as corporate houses retrench expensive staff in search of more capital intensive production methods.

Due to the fall in revenues, the government has to reduce the public services and social security measures. Tax competition among the jurisdictions not only leads to reduced revenues but also results in an increase in illegal evasion and cross border shopping. Even though a government legalises the individuals to import commodities, it is generally impossible to enforce the border trade as the individuals import from low tax jurisdictions and sell it illegally without paying the taxes in high tax jurisdictions. These illegal smugglers will not pay the corporate or personal income taxes and the local retail vendors too are affected as they stand to lose a substantial business, leading to reduced government revenues from corporate and personal income taxes. "When jurisdictions differ in size, the smaller ones have advantages in capturing some tax base from the larger ones by under cutting their higher tax rate and by setting an average tax rate as a harmonization measure, it can always be beneficial for all the jurisdictions in terms of revenue maximization". [12] Hence, the rationale for harmonization aims at revenue stabilization from evasion point of view.

2.9.2 Importance of National Objectives: Generally, in federations, the decentralization of functions and resources are aimed at attaining certain national objectives such as fostering economic growth, revenue sustainability to finance fiscal deficits, equitable regional development, high public provision etc., considering the whole country as one unit. Accordingly, in its implementation, federal policies are evolved in tune with the federal objectives and it has overriding powers over the sub-national policies even to rationalize the imposition of uniformity among the sub-national governments considering that an efficient allocation of resources becomes a matter of concern for the federation.

Assignment of taxes at different levels of government is one of the policy instruments for achieving redistribution equity. For making equity as a federal objective, centre is the only level where all the citizens can be treated equally and this may be disturbed if the states have different methods for redistribution. In terms of efficiency, tax differentials among the sub-national governments lead to unequal regional development as the industry and business developments are attracted towards the low tax jurisdictions, implying the failure of redistributional equity among the people of different jurisdictions and calling for the harmonization of taxes, as it promotes regional growth and distribution goals.

2.9.3 Administrative Efficiency: In terms of efficiency, federal governments are better equipped than the sub-national governments in running the tax administration and managing the huge databases more efficiently, resulting in collection of taxes at a lower cost and it is convenient for the tax payers also in terms of uniformity of tax procedures throughout the federation. Decentralization of revenue collection often tends to increase the cost of collection and compliance, leading to diseconomies of scale. Tax avoidance and evasion are also bound to increase with decentralization as the lower level governments lack personnel and logistics to administer the taxes efficiently.

Even though centralization of tax powers are preferable in terms of efficiency, revenue stability and equity considerations, it certainly undermines the fiscal autonomy of sub-national governments that go against the subsidiarity principle which stipulates that the governments which are close to the people should be assigned the functions that can be efficiently discharged by them. But Simon James (2002), suggested, "the concept of subsidiarity could be more helpful in progress towards successful harmonization". Hence, assignment is not the only solution and there are problems that can be tackled satisfactorily through policy coordination, which aims to prevent distortions and inequities arising from tax differentials without impairing the desired size of public sector and the taxation structure.

2.9.4 Increasing Mobility of Capital and Labour: During the last two decades, many countries world over have initiated many steps towards elimination of investment barriers such as decontrolling of foreign currency exchange, deregulation of financial markets, buying of foreign securities and allowing foreigners to purchase domestic securities and companies. A report published by the International Monetary Fund (August 2001) on capital markets has shown that foreign direct investment flows rapidly grew from US$ 204 billion during the year 1990 to US$ 1.3 trillion dollars during the year 2001 and the portfolio investments flows increased from US$ 219 billion during the year 1990 to US$ 1.4 trillion during the year 2000. In order to attract more foreign direct investments, many countries in recent years have initiated several reform measures to get their economic fundamentals right by establishing a stable currency, trusted legal laws and a liquid transparent financial market.

As a result, taxation policies became important instruments thereby influencing the investment and the investors became sensitive to tax differentials. Many studies instituted by various agencies have confirmed that taxation is one of the main factors influencing foreign direct investment, corporate borrowing, transfer pricing, dividend and royalty payments and countries with 10 percent higher taxes attracted only less than 30 percent American foreign investments. Countries with lower tax rates received higher investments. Within the European Economic Union, four countries namely Ireland, Netherlands, Luxembourg and Switzerland with lower taxes attracted nearly 40 percent of American foreign direct investment than other countries. On the contrary, countries with higher tax rates such as Germany and Sweden lost substantial outflow of its savings to other European countries with lower taxes.

Under globalization, multinational corporations hire skilled workers from different countries and this mobility of labour has increased over the years—as it is possible to assess the job opportunities through internet, reduced travel and communication costs, reduced emigration restrictions, working for a foreign country while residing at home due to advanced technology, regional trade agreements between various countries and increase in the cap of immigration limits for skilled workers. This mobility of labour between the countries causes brain drain as workers with higher incomes may be attracted towards a low taxed jurisdiction.

With elimination of internal migration in European Union in 1992, skilled workers specialising in technology and finance moved to London from other countries within the European Union where there are low taxes and more opportunities. Similarly, Ireland with huge reduction in corporate and income taxation attracted more than 20,000 immigrants annually and a also saw a drastic fall in emigration. Hence, tax competition among the jurisdictions in terms of financial inflows and skilled labour leads to distortions and other harmful effects and hence harmonization of taxes becomes essential.

2.10 Effects of Tax Harmonization

Even though tax harmonization eliminates distortions due to consumption and production, it would be better to assess its impact on welfare aspects empirically. Studies conducted by the European Commission on the basis of destination-based commodity taxation, focused on the impediments to the creation of a unified single market, reveal that tax harmonization leads to welfare in three ways, viz. abolition of border controls, relocation of industries and the realization of economies to scale in production.

2.10.1 Abolition of Border Controls: A study conducted by the European Commission in 1988 shows that tax rate differentials are less important than technical standards and regulations, administrative barriers, frontier formalities and freight transport regulations. The cost of savings to firms due to tax rate differentials ranged from a moderate 1 percent to 3 percent of total trade within the European Union and contributed a nominal 0.2 percent to 0.3 percent to the GDP.

2.10.2 Relocation of Industries: As the value added tax (VAT) was levied for both sales taxes and excise duties based on the destination principle in the entire European Community, distortion in the location of industries did not arise as the VAT ensured uniformity in tax rates.

2.10.3 Realization of Economies to Scale: Even though destination principle does provides opportunities to tax the imports, a study conducted by the European Commission in 1988 showed that realization of economies to scale ranged between 1 percent to 63 percent and the welfare gains from realisation of economies to scale ranged from 1 percent to 4 percent of the GDP as the abolition of tax barriers stimulated confidence among the firms and individuals as the uncertainty of taxation policies reduced.

However, a study conducted by Pearson and Smith (1990), revealed that United Kingdom, a member country of European Union, suffered in its consumption pattern due to introduction of taxation for zero-rated items such as food, books and newspapers, children's cloth and a reduced tax for alcoholic drinks leading to an increased sale (39 percent) of alcoholic drinks, reduced sale of 3 percent for food items, reduced sale of 12 percent in petrol, and a reduced sale of 5 percent of fuel, leading to a fall of 1.9 billion pounds of tax revenue from alcoholic drinks, questioning the very process of harmonization. Hence, harmonization reduces distortions in consumption at the international level or at the federation level but increases the internal ones if the new tax structure does not meet the country's preferences and the overall welfare effects will be a loss for the member country state. [13]

Generally, taxation is used to raise revenue to meet the public expenditures in different countries/states, which have different public expenditure needs and different tax bases and different preferences for public goods. Harmonization does not imply uniformity unless the enforcement of tax laws is applied uniformly in all the constituent units. It should consider the welfare effects as the subsidies can also change the actual effect of taxation and only if the value of the welfare is the same across the jurisdictions, neutrality is ensured by uniform taxation. Hence, uniform taxation alone is not sufficient for increasing the welfare if the constituent units differ from each other in terms of welfare. However, some degree of tax diversity may be allowed.

2.11 Tax Co-ordination

As complete harmonization of taxes leads to equalization of effective tax rates, it may involve a substantial loss of welfare. Tax co-ordination tries to evolve a tax structure that aims to avoid distortions and externalities arising from tax competition without impairing fiscal autonomy and leading to a reduction in the size of the public sector.

In the absence of market power, destination principle fails due to cross border shopping, leading to the lowering of taxes and having a negative impact on revenue of the jurisdictions on others rates. By setting a minimum tax, downward decrease in tax rates can be avoided as a co-ordination measure since jurisdictions choosing a higher rate lose a part of revenue and the jurisdiction choosing a lower rate gains revenue at the cost of others.

In the presence of market power, tax competition leads to lower taxes on exports and higher taxes on imports. By setting a higher tax rate for exports and vice-versa, all the constituent units of a federation can improve welfare as a whole. But a more practical approach would be dealing with each of the major taxes and their possible distortions and externalities and how best they are tackled by different countries to create a common market and achieving neutrality in taxation to provide a better picture.

2.12 Tax Rate Convergence

Recent advances in tax harmonization theory shows that tax harmonization, even under origin principle, can lead to actual and Pareto-improving provided the harmonization converges towards the average tax of the jurisdictions. Unified single market approach reduces distortions in tax system, abolishes border controls, tariff barriers and protective devices between jurisdictions who do not meet the conditions for a fair trade. Michael Keen (2002), pointed out that zero-rating goods claimed to be exported to another member state/country receives refund for inputs and are subsequently sold in the same jurisdiction without tax being paid. This kind of tax avoidance reduces the tax revenues and it is likely to arise in any federal country which implements sub-national value added taxes where inter-state export is a major concern. [14]

To avoid these tax evasions, Keen (1987), established, "a harmonization reform using a standard model of international trade, in which tax rates are the weighted average of pre-existing destination-based commodity taxes with weights being the different demand responses in each jurisdiction, generated a potential Pareto improvement. [15] The direct implication of this harmonization reform is the efficient allocation of commodities from consumers with low marginal valuation to consumers with high marginal valuation. Keen (1989), established conditions for strict Pareto improvement keeping in view the pre-existence of protective/impulses such as the higher revenue tax on the imported commodities. [16]

rtions in efficient allocation of production and con...nption and the latter results in the encroachment of tax base of one jurisdiction by another and ultimately impairing the growth of the federal economy. Hence, there is a need for tax harmonization and co-ordination among the lower levels of government in a federation. However, by adopting uniform tax rates across the jurisdictions by preventing inefficiencies in production and consumption and through cross border movements, tax harmonization can be achieved irrespective of the taxation principle, leading to the neutrality of tax systems.

Endnotes

1. Oates, W.E. (1999), "An Essay on Fiscal Federalism", *Journal of Economic Literature*, Vol. 37, American Economic Association, Nashville, Tennessee, 3, September 1999, pp. 1120-1149.
2. Ussher, Kitty (2001), "The Spectre of Tax Harmonization", available at: www.cer.org.uk/pdf/p165taxharmonization.pdf.
3. Nodir, Khudarbergarov (2000), "A Proposed Framework of Analysis for a Single Economic and Yap Su Fei Environment: Pre-requisites, Impact and Analysis in the Context of European Integration", FEA, Working Paper 2000-2005, University of Malaya, Kuala Lumpur, Malaysia.
4. Edwards, Christ and Derugy (2002), "International Tax Competition", Annual Report, The Fraser Institute, Vancouver, Canada, pp. 43-55.
5. Robin Broadway, (1998), "Fiscal Federation: Dimensions of Tax Reform in Developing Countries", Washington, D.C.: The World Bank.
6. Sorensen, Peter Birch (2001), "Tax Coordination in European Union: What are the Issues?", *Swedish Economic Policy Review*, Vol. 8, The Economic Council of Sweden, Stockholm, Sweden, pp. 143-195.
7. Mclure, Jr. Charles (2001), "Tax Harmonization, Fiscal Federation and Regional Economic Integration: International Experience and Lessons from Brazil", prepared for an international seminar on tax systems and competitiveness organized by Brazilian National Confederation on Industry

Brazil, May 28, 2001, *Tax Notes International*, Vol. 22, Tax Analysts, Washington, US, pp. 2861-2869.

8. Mintz and Tulkens (1986), "Commodity Tax Competition between Member States of a Federation: Equilibrium and Efficiency", *Journal of Public Economics*, Vol. 29, Elsevier Toronto, Canada, pp. 133-172.
9. Keen and Kostaginnasis (2004), "Tax Competition in Federations and Welfare Consequences of Decentralization", International Monetary Fund, Washington, available at: www.warwick.ac.uk/fac/soc/csgr/research/workingpapers/2004/wp14704.pdf.
10. Mario, Alfano and Mossimo Salzano Rosario (2001), "Tax Competition in an Open Border Scenario: An Evolutionary Game Theoretic Approach", University of Salerno, Federico Caffe Centre Research Report, 1/2000, Fisciano, Italy, available at: www.ruc.dk/federico/publications/SALZANO1_2000.pdf.
11. Rao, M.G. (1993), "Impediments to Internal Trade and Allocative Distortions in India", working paper of National Institute of Public Finance and Policy, New Delhi.
12. Gandelman, Neston Murillo and Hernandex Ruben (2002), "Tax Competition and Tax Harmonization with Evasion", Federal Reserve Bank of St. Louis, U.S., available at: research.stlouised.org/wp/2002/2002-015.pdf.
13. Debonis, Valeria (1997), "Regional Integration and Commodity Tax Harmonization", The World Bank Policy Research Working Paper 1848, available at: www.worldbank.org/research/trade/pdf/wp1848.pdf.
14. Keen, M.J. (2002), "Some International Issues in Commodity Taxation", *Swedish Economic Policy Review*, Vol. 9, The Economic Council of Sweden, Stockholm, Sweden, pp. 9-39.
15. Keen, M.J. (1987), "Welfare Effects of Commodity Tax Harmonization", *Journal of Public Economics*, Vol. 33, Elsevier, Toronto, Canada, pp. 107-114.
16. Keen, M.J. (1989), "Pareto-improving Indirect Tax Harmonization", *European Economic Review*, Vol. 33, Elsevier, Toronto, Canada, pp. 1-12.
17. Delipalla, Sofia (1997), "Commodity Tax Harmonization and Public Goods", *Journal of Public Economics*, Vol. 63, Elsevier, Toronto, Canada, pp. 447-466.

18. Lockwood, Ben (1996), "Can Commodity Tax Harmonization be Pareto-improving When Government Supply Goods?", *Journal of International Economics*, Vol. 43, Elsevier, Toronto, Canada, pp. 387-408.
19. Lopez, Garcia and Miguel Angel (1996), "The Origin Principle and the Welfare Gains from Indirect Tax Harmonization", *International Tax and Public Finance*, Vol. 3, Elsevier, Toronto, Canada, pp. 83-93.
20. Lahiri and Raimondos (1998), "Public Good Provision and Welfare Effects of Indirect Tax Harmonization", *Journal of Public Economics*, Vol. 67, Elsevier, Toronto, Canada, pp. 253-267.
21. Lockwood, de Meza and Myles (1994), "Tax Harmonization and the Origin Principle", *Economic Letters*, Vol. 71, Elsevier, Toronto, Canada, pp. 111-115.
22. Lucas, Vander (2000), "Tax Harmonization and Public Good Provision in the Origin Principle", Universidade Catolica de Brazilia, Department of Economics, discussion paper, available at: www.unb.br/face/eco/cpe/TD/310maio2004Vander.pdf.
23. Kotsogiannis, Christos Lopez-Garnia, Miquel D.Myles and Gareth Angel (2003), "The Origin Principle, Tax Harmonization and Public Goods", Spanish Science and Technology System Project No. BEC 20000415 and the Catalan Government Science Network Project No. SGR 2001-160.

3

Excise Duties

3.1 Historical Background

Excise duty is a tax on goods manufactured and collected from the manufacturer on the manufacture of excisable goods irrespective of whether the goods manufactured are sold or not and ends at the production point. It is one of the oldest, important and largest sources of revenue for the Government of India.

Excise duty was levied in 1884 by the erstwhile British regime for the first time at a rate of 5 percent on cotton yarn and later converted into an excise duty on cloths to provide a competitive edge to the Lancashire cloth in the Indian market. Later in 1917, a levy was imposed on motor spirit in order to curb its domestic consumption and increase the supply to the defence forces engaged in war. In 1934, excise duty was levied to sugar, matches and steel ingots. During 1940s, tyres and tubes, tobacco, coffee and tea were brought under excise taxation mainly to finance wars. Cigarettes and mill made cloth were also within the tax net in 1948 and 1949 respectively. Lakdawala and Nambiar (1972) commented that the early stage of Indian excise system had a basic purpose of either to restrict the consumption of scarce resources or to compensate the loss of revenue resulting from custom duties on import of parallel commodities. [1]

The Central Government, under the Constitution was empowered to levy excise duties on all manufactured products except liquor, opium, Indian hemp and other narcotic drugs which are under the purview of the state governments and the proceeds were shared between the Central and state governments on the basis of the recommendations of Finance Commissions constituted quinquenially. Over the years, the revenue from excise duties expanded remarkably due to the rapid increase in industrial production, the periodic revision of excise duty rates and bringing more and more commodities under taxation. Table 3.1 gives the history of commodities covered under the excise system.

Table 3.1: Coverage of Commodities

Period	Commodities
Up to 1949	Motor spirit, kerosene, sugar, steel ingots, matches, ingots, tyres, unmanufactured tobacco, vegetable product, coffee, tea, cigarettes and cotton fabrics.
1950-54	Soap, rayon, cement, footwear.
1955-59	Paints, paper, woollen fabrics, electric batteries, bulbs, fans, refined diesel oil, furnace oil, vegetable non-essential oils, synthetic fibres and yarn, motor cars, asphalt, bitumen and tar.
1960-64	Silk fabrics, pig iron, aluminium, tin plates, internal combustion engines, electric motors, cycles, cinematograph films, motor vehicles, soda ash, caustic soda, glycerin, dyestuffs, cosmetics, medicines, plastics, cellophane, cotton yarn, woollen yarn, glass and glassware, chinaware, copper, zinc, refrigerating machinery, wireless receiving sets, petroleum products, acids, gases, rubber products, plywood, jute manufactures, asbestos, cement products, iron and steel products, electric cables, gramophones, sodium silicate.
1965-69	Lead, synthetic organic products, organic surface-active agents (other than soap), confectionery, textile fabrics, impregnated steel, furniture, crown corks, preserved food, fertilizers, power driven pumps, domestic electrical appliances, pilfer proof caps, wool tops.
1970-74	Food products, aerated waters, glucose, chemicals, synthetic rubber, office machines, metal containers, safe and strong boxes, maida, lubricating oils and greases, calcined petroleum coke, linoleum, ready-made garments, typewriter and similar ribbons, mosaic tiles, motor starters, electricity supply meters, motors vehicles parts, fork lift trucks, cinematograph projectors, cameras, rolling bearings, welding electrodes, coated abrasive, bolts, nuts, screws, zip fasteners, pressure cookers, vacuum flasks, playing cards, camphor, menthol, adhesive tapes, silk yarn, jute yarn, textile fabrics, tool tips, wire ropes, carbon black, rubber processing chemicals, smoking mixtures, toothpaste, electrical stampings, tape recorders, cutting tools, permanent magnets.

Contd...

1975-80	All other goods not elsewhere specified, chewing tobacco, snuff, graphite electrodes, starch, mineral fibres and yarn, computers, acetylene gas Polishes, watches, weighing, machinery, tools, musical systems, flax yarn, coal, electricity, *hookah* tobacco, floor coverings, locks, tooth brushes, molasses.
1981-85	Petroleum gases, television image and sound recorders and reproducers, television cameras, Electronic machines for games of skill or chance, articles used for sound or sound and image recording, pan masala, organic chemicals, marbles in the form of blocks, slabs and tiles, travel goods namely briefcases, variety bags, and variety cases all sorts.

Source: Central Excise Tariff as on 25.07.1985, pp. 583-585.

The Taxation Enquiry Commission (TEC) (1953-54) laid the foundation for the future expansion of commodity coverage and taxation and observed that to raise substantial revenue, it was imperative to tax not only the luxuries but also necessities and even goods within the purview of Essential Goods Act under Article 286 of the Constitution. [2] As per the recommendations of the TEC, commodity coverage expanded over the years as given in Table 3.1. Hence, excise duty structure that started with few commodities ultimately covered all inputs and final goods. In the 1975-76 Budget, one percent excise duty was levied on all manufactured products. The indirect taxation committee headed by L.K. Jha commented, "In effect, what we are having today is an extended excise system which is tending towards universal coverage of industrial goods". [3]

3.2 Types of Excise Duty

Under Entry 84 of List I of the Seventh Schedule (Article 246) of the Indian Constitution, the Union Government is empowered to levy excise duty on tobacco and other goods manufactured in India except alcoholic liquors, opium, Indian hemp and other narcotic drugs. Under the provisions of the Constitution, various types of excise duty are levied by the central government such as basic excise duty, additional duties in lieu of sales tax and cesses.

3.2.1 Basic Excise Duty: The duty imposed under central

Excises and Salt Act, 1944 is known as basic excise duty and it may be imposed according to the ad valorem or specific rates depending on the excisable goods. In addition, there is a special excise duty on select products.

3.2.2 Additional Duties in Lieu of Sales Tax: These are the levies imposed under Additional Duties of Excise Act, 1957, entitled to levy additional duties of excise on textiles, sugar and tobacco in place of sales tax levied by state government and the proceeds are distributed to the states as per the directions of the Finance Commissions and it was decided by the National Development Council in 1956. As the duties are collected by the Central government, these commodities bear a uniform tax burden throughout the country and facilitate easy movement of goods within the country, less tax evasion due to the collection at the manufacturing stage, low cost of collection and high compliance. This can be taken as a step towards tax harmonization and coordinated commodity tax system in the country.

3.2.3 Cesses: Cesses are levied in addition to basic excise duties on selected commodities under separate enactments in order to encourage selected industries and finance the research and development activities.

In addition to the above duties, there are two other duties such as the additional duty on motor spirit (petrol) and diesel and additional duties of excise (textile and textile articles) on fibres, yarns and fabrics to subsidise controlled cloth scheme.

For the levy of central excise duty, "manufacture" is defined in Section 2(f) of Central Excise Act as any process resulting in new articles that can be marketable.

3.3 Structure of Excise Administration

The Central Board of Excise and Customs is the topmost body under the Ministry of Finance, monitoring the assessment and collection of excise duty through its large network of offices well entrenched throughout the country. At the bottom, there is a range office, which is directly associated with the assessment and collection of excise duty. A group of range offices are being administered by the divisional offices, which in turn are being administered by excise collectorates under the control of central excise board.

In addition, there are directorates for training, inspection, audit, anti-evasion and the directorate of statistics to offer ancillary support to personnel involved in assessment and collection. There are various methods in assessment and collection of central excise, such as the physical control system, self-removal procedure and the compound levy scheme.

Every manufacturer needs to be registered before commencing production. Each manufacturer is given an ECCN (Excise and Customs Corporation Nomenclature) based permanent account number (PAN) by the income tax Department. But, SSI units, whose turnover is less than ₹ 1 crore, do not need any registration. But they have to file a declaration when their clearances reach a level of ₹ 10 lakh, that is less than the exemption limit. In addition, manufacturers have to file a classification declaration giving details of products and rate of duty and give a price declaration even if the sale is through related persons, or where price is not the sole consideration. Manufacturers have to pay the duty every fortnight for clearances between 1st-15th, by 20th, and for clearances between 16th-30th, by 5th of next month.

For March, there is a separate provision declaration for the second fortnight of March. In case of cash payment, it can be only through nominated banks. SSI units can make monthly payments but by 15th of the next month. Finally, every manufacturer has to file a monthly RT-12 return of assessment (quarterly for SSI units) and monthly Cenvat return of Cenvat input credit availment. No statutory records are prescribed but the records kept must cover all production, use of inputs, sales, purchases etc.

A self-removal procedure is allowed though checks by officers and conducted through scrutiny of assessment returns, inspection/visits by officers, audit and anti-evasion measures.

With liberalisation and abolition of statutory needs, audit

has an increasing role to play. For this, there is a need to have trained staff and developed techniques of audit selection so as to focus on suspect units. Also, anti-evasion needs to be strengthened with stress on intelligence gathering.

3.4 Methods of Excise Duty Collection

3.4.1 Physical Control System: Until 1968, the excise department under which the production of industries was personally verified by the excise staff and the excise levy was collected on the spot, this procedure was adopted. Interestingly, this procedure still applies for cigarettes.

3.4.2 Self-removal Procedure: In this method, the assessee is permitted to take clearances on his own assessment of duty liability without physical verification by the excise staff. Instead, he has to obtain his classification list approved by the excise department and further he has to submit a price list charged along with the discounts and deductions. Major products are covered under this method since 1968.

3.4.3 Compounded Levy Scheme: Under this scheme, a lump sum amount is paid based on some installation such as number of spindles in textile mills and the manufacturer is free from excise procedures and he is required only to maintain the record of spindles in his mill. This provides advantages to small-scale manufacturers as they get relief from the ordeals of normal excise procedures. Among the various procedures listed above, physical control system appears to be the right one as the excise staff posted at the manufacturing site, physically verifies the production, storage and clearance of excisable goods. But this system was abolished by the government in 1968 due to sustained campaign launched by the industrial lobby and the government succumbed to pressure notwithstanding the recommendations of the Taxation Enquiry Commission, which turned down the plea.

Under the self-removable procedure, excise duty is collected based on trust and belief placed on the manufacturers and became prone to high tax evasion and even the Central Excise Review

Committee failed to quantify the volume of evasion. In 1986, a new Harmonized System of Nomenclature (HSN) classifying the commodities was introduced replacing the old system. In the new system, excise tariff schedule covered 137 tariff items and with the sub-items taken together, there were more than 355 main classifications. The Indian Standard Institution designs the definitions and description of commodities and Customs Corporation Council gives the explanatory notes. In addition, there is a method called collection at point of consumption, which applies to molasses where users pay the duty and another production-based levy which applies to independent processors such as in the case of processing of fabrics.

3.5 Exemptions

The Indian excise system is supposed to serve a number of socio-economic obligations such as improvement of small industries, support for family planning measures, etc. Accordingly, excise exemptions/concessions were declared from time to time through government notifications. There is a multiplicity of exemptions. Though the tariff rates are prescribed in the schedule, the effective rates can be lower because of exemption. The types of exemptions are as follows:

1. Exemption/concessional rates for small-scale industry (SSI).
2. Specified products of village industry, and marketed with the assistance of KVIC.
3. Specified goods made in rural areas—areas comprised in a village as defined in the land revenue records.
4. Specified goods supplied to public funded research institutions, non-commercial institutes and universities.
5. Goods produced by ordinance factories and defence related exemptions.
6. Goods donated to National Defence Fund.
7. Specified goods produced without the aid of power.
8. A number of food products—khandsari sugar, bread, spices, coffee, certain unbranded food items.

9. Fertilizers, cereals, edible oils.
10. Aircraft, ship, boat etc.

3.6 Excise Duty Rates

In the early days of excise system before 1986-87, excise duty in India had multiplicity of rates due to various considerations which often caused confusion. The rate of most food products was fixed at 15 percent and on butter and vegetable oils it was fixed at 10 percent ad valorem. Sugar bears a specific duty of ₹ 24 per quintal. Pharmaceutical products bear a duty rate ranging between 12 and 15 percent ad valorem.

Essential domestic durables are taxed moderately ad valorem with rates of duty ranging from 10 percent on footwear, 15 percent for clocks and watches and 30 percent on washing machines. Semi-luxuries such as refrigerators and tape recorders bear 20 percent and television sets 40 percent. Luxury items are taxed heavily such as cosmetics and air conditioners which bear 105 and 110 percent of duty respectively.

Tobacco items bear the highest rates of duty. Fine variety of cigars is taxed at 75 percent whereas smoking mixtures bear a duty of 225 percent. Excise duty on non-filter cigarettes of size up to 70mm was fixed at ₹ 150 per 1,000 cigarettes. Filter cigarettes are taxed in four slabs, viz. ₹ 200 for cigarettes up to 70 mm, ₹ 300 over 70 mm and up to 75 mm, ₹ 400 over 75 mm and up to 85 mm and ₹ 600 over 85 mm and up to 100 mm.

Petroleum products bear specific rates with motor spirit, high speed diesel, and kerosene and furnace oil taxed at ₹ 2,750, ₹ 1,000, ₹ 500 and ₹ 127 respectively per kilolitre. To meet the unprecedented after effects of drought in 1987, a surcharge by way of special duty was levied at the rate of 1/20th of the basic duty of excise on all products except commodities of mass consumption viz., sugar, matches, cotton fabrics, vanaspati, refined vegetable oil, tea, coffee and kerosene.

In the beginning of excise system in India, specific rates were favoured for administrative reasons. Later on, during the 1970s, a large number items were shifted from specific to ad valorem rates such as cement, vegetable products, electric fans, lighting bulbs and tubes, soaps, soda, sodium silicate, cotton fabrics and paper. 1980s saw the halt of shift to ad valorem rates due to unprecedented spurt in litigation pertained to disputes over classification and valuation of goods for the purpose of excise duties. To minimise tax evasion and tax avoidance, basic duty changed from ad valorem to ad valorem-cum-specific or specific rate on a number of commodities. Even though economic analysis favours ad valorem rates so as to keep in pace with inflation, specific rates are preferred for administrative considerations and it seems that the shift from ad valorem to specific rates has been forced upon by the Government through manipulative tactics and lobbying by the industry. An examination of the Central Excise Tariff Act, 1955 shows that out of 91 chapters listed, 61 chapters bear ad valorem rates, 7 chapters specific rates, 19 chapters ad valorem and specific rates and the last 4 chapters nil rate of duty.

3.7 Revenue Importance

It is obvious from Tables 3.2, 3.3 and 3.4 about the revenue importance of union excises duties in the Indian tax system. Revenue from union excise duties has posted phenomenal growth over the years. Its relative share has gone up to 56.3 percent during 1970-71 and subsequently declined to 19.6 percent during 2015-16. In terms of GDP, its relative share was the highest (4.5 percent) during 1980-81 and later declined to 2.5 percent during 2015-16. The declining trend noticed in Union excise duty is due to fallout of the gradual implementation of tax reform measures since 1991 by the Central Government.

As shown in Table 3.2, growth of revenues since 1950-51 has been phenomenal due to additional coverage of commodities and tax rate revisions. When the commodity coverage reached the saturation point, tariff hikes become difficult. Therefore, excise revenue would depend mainly on the increase in production of excisable goods, which in turn, depend on the development of the economy in general and industrialization in particular and it was between 1965-66 and 1975-76 that the growth of revenue was significant at 35.9 percent. [4]

Table 3.2: Trends in Tax Revenues of the Central Government

(₹ crore)

Year	Corporation Tax	Income Tax	Customs Duty	Excise Duty	Service Tax	Total
1950-51	40	132	157	68	0	397
1960-61	111	166	170	414	0	861
1970-71	371	473	524	1,759	0	3,127
1980-81	1,310	1,506	3,409	6,500	0	12,725
1990-91	5,335	5,371	20,644	24,514	0	55,864
2000-01	35,696	31,764	47,542	68,526	3,000	1,86,528
2004-05	82,680	49,259	57,611	99,125	14,200	3,02,875
2005-06	1,03,573	66,239	64,215	1,12,000	23,000	3,69,027
2006-07	1,44,318	80,409	86,327	1,17,612	37,598	4,66,264
2007-08	1,92,911	1,11,820	1,04,119	1,23,611	51,302	5,83,763
2008-09	2,13,395	1,06,075	99,879	1,08,613	60,941	5,88,903
2009-10	2,44,725	1,22,417	83,324	1,02,991	58,422	6,11,879
2010-11	2,98,688	1,39,102	1,35,813	1,37,701	71,016	7,82,320
2011-12	3,22,816	1,64,525	1,49,328	1,44,901	97,509	8,79,079
2012-13	3,58,874	1,99,933	1,64,853	1,71,315	1,32,697	10,27,672
2013-14	4,19,520	2,40,922	1,87,308	1,96,805	1,80,141	12,24,696
2014-15	4,28,924	2,58,325	1,88,016	1,88,127	1,67,969	12,31,361
2015-16	4,52,969	2,91,653	2,09,500	2,83,353	2,10,000	14,47,475
2016-17 (B.E.)	4,93,923	3,45,775	2,30,000	3,17,860	2,31,000	16,18,558

Source: Budget Documents, Ministry of Finance, Government of India.

From Table 3.5, it is apparent that in spite of a universal coverage of commodities under excise system, only a limited number of commodities viz. petroleum products, iron and steel, tobacco products, cement, motor vehicles, chemical products, plastics and machinery have been yielding more than

90 percent of the revenue and a larger number of commodities accrue negligible or meagre amount of revenue. In view of this, the administration can concentrate more on high yielding commodities and if the revenue leakage is plugged on these commodities, more revenue can be collected with reduction in cost of collections.

Table 3.3: Relative Shares of Various Central Taxes

(percent)

Year	Corporation Tax	Income Tax	Customs Duty	Excise Duty	Service Tax
1950-51	10.1	33.2	39.5	17.1	0.0
1960-61	12.9	19.3	19.7	48.1	0.0
1970-71	11.9	15.1	16.8	56.3	0.0
1980-81	10.3	11.8	26.8	51.1	0.0
1990-91	9.5	9.6	37.0	43.9	0.0
2000-01	19.2	17.1	25.5	36.8	1.6
2001-02	19.8	17.3	21.8	39.3	1.8
2005-06	28.1	17.9	17.4	30.4	6.2
2006-07	31.0	17.2	18.5	25.2	8.1
2007-08	33.0	19.2	17.8	21.2	8.8
2008-09	36.2	18.0	17.0	18.4	10.3
2009-10	40.0	20.0	13.6	16.8	9.5
2010-11	38.2	17.8	17.4	17.6	9.1
2011-12	36.7	18.7	17.0	16.5	11.1
2012-13	34.9	19.5	16.0	16.7	12.9
2013-14	34.3	19.7	15.3	16.1	14.7
2014-15	34.8	21.0	15.3	15.3	13.6
2015-16	31.3	20.1	14.5	19.6	14.5
2016-17 (B.E.)	30.5	21.4	14.2	19.6	14.3

3.8 Deficiencies

Though the total revenue did increase for the period between 1951 and 1986, the central excise system confronted certain deficiencies. The major deficiencies faced by the excise system were as under:

1. Cascading input taxation.
2. Complex rate structure.
3. Exclusion of services.
4. Additional duties of excise in lieu of sales tax.

Table 3.4: Central Government Tax Revenue by Source as Percentage of GDP

Year	Corporation Tax	Income Tax	Customs Duty	Excise Duty	Service Tax	Tax/GDP Ratio
1950-51	0.4	1.3	1.6	0.7	0.0	4.0
1960-61	0.6	1.0	1.0	2.4	0.0	5.0
1970-71	0.8	1.0	1.1	3.9	0.0	6.8
1980-81	0.9	1.0	2.4	4.5	0.0	8.9
1990-91	1.0	1.0	3.6	4.3	0.0	9.9
2000-01	1.7	1.5	2.3	3.3	0.1	8.9
2001-02	1.6	1.4	1.9	3.5	0.2	8.6
2002-03	2.3	1.5	1.8	3.3	0.2	9.8
2003-04	2.3	1.5	1.8	3.3	0.3	9.2
2004-05	2.7	1.6	1.8	3.3	0.5	9.9
2005-06	3.1	1.9	1.5	3.5	0.7	10.7
2006-07	3.4	1.9	2.0	2.7	0.9	10.9
2007-08	3.9	2.2	2.1	2.5	1.0	11.7
2008-09	3.8	1.9	1.8	1.9	1.1	10.5
2009-10	3.8	1.9	1.3	1.6	0.9	9.4
2010-11	3.8	1.8	1.7	1.8	0.9	10.0
2011-12	3.6	1.8	1.7	1.6	1.1	9.8
2012-13	3.6	2.0	1.7	1.7	1.3	10.4
2013-14	3.7	2.2	1.7	1.8	1.6	10.9
2014-15	5.2	2.9	1.9	2.3	1.5	13.8
2015-16	5.7	3.5	2.0	2.5	1.7	15.4

Source: Budget Documents, Ministry of Finance, Government of India.

3.8.1 Cascading Input Taxation: An excise duty levied on inputs feeds into the price of the input. A manufacturer who uses the input to produce an output incorporates the value of input while fixing the output price. When the output is taxed, the value of output along with the input, which is paid earlier, is also taxed again. This "tax on tax" is called cascading. As a result, the production cost increases as producers and middlemen require large working capital to raise inventories of inputs. Finally, the price of the finished goods will cost more due to the taxation of inputs and the consumers have to bear the burden. As excises are levied on inputs as well as on the final output, a gap arises between the nominal and a cumulative rate which complicates the proper evaluation of equity criterion. Estimating incidence of excise taxation becomes difficult, as it is difficult to estimate the cumulative levy on finished products.

Table 3.5: List of Commodities Yielding Revenue of More than ₹ 1,000 crore in 2014-15

S. No.	Commodity	Revenue (₹ crore)	Percentage Share
1.	Petroleum products	88,065	52.6
2.	Iron and steel	17,342	10.4
3.	Tobacco products	16,050	9.6
4.	Cement	10,308	6.2
5.	Motor vehicles	8,363	5.0
6.	Chemical products	4,845	2.9
7.	Plastics	4,298	2.6
8.	Machinery	3,761	2.2
9.	Others	14,267	8.5
	Total (1 to 8)	1,53,032	91.5
	Total (all commodities)	1,67,299	100.0

Source: Comptroller and Auditor General's Report, 2014-15.

Moreover, input taxation promotes vertical integration of industry, which is harmful for the small-scale sector. Further, input of taxation fails to distinguish between essential and non-essential goods. The Indirect Taxation Enquiry Committee pointed out, "whatever is used for further production by manufacturers, who are themselves subject to tax, should be given relief since, for the same product, the consumers will pay the tax at the appropriate rate". [5] Under such systems, all units of goods would bear taxation, as the taxation on inputs would be eligible for a set-off and there would not arise any divergence between the nominal and cumulative rates.

The Indirect Taxation Committee (ITC) (1977) stated that the biggest weakness of the indirect taxation in India was the cost cascading effects. With widespread taxation of inputs by more than one authority, it is difficult to control the incidence on final products.

3.8.2 Complex Rate Structure: Existence of numerous tax rates under a single classification causes confusion such as tobacco items which have a number of tax rates for different types of its products such as filter cigarettes, non-filter cigarettes, cigars, chewing tobacco, etc. Petroleum products have different tax rates for motor spirit, high speed diesel, kerosene and furnace oil. The Indirect Taxation Committee (1977) found a plethora of rates on similar commodities arbitrarily fixed primarily on revenue considerations. The Indirect Taxation Committee (1978) recommended a set of four excise rates capped at 10, 20, 30 and 40 percent with some exceptional goods. There was a wide variation even among these rates in response to the lobbying by pressure groups, leading to anarchy of rates.

Venkatappiah Committee that was instituted to study the complex tax rate structure pointed out that there were 300 statutory basic rates of excise duties on all excisable commodities, which ultimately resulted in 2,000 effective rates through administrative notifications. Textile items alone accounted for 200 effective rates. Moreover, some tax rates were specific, some others ad valorem and a few partly specific and partly ad valorem. Excise duty on pharmaceuticals ranged from 12 percent to 15 percent. Most essential household articles were taxed between 10 percent to 110 percent. As specific duties accounted for a major share in the excise duty structure, the excise system was less progressive and inelastic to inflation.

3.8.3 Exclusion of Services: As the Constitution of India empowered the governments to levy taxes on goods without mentioning the services, taxing services under excise or sales taxation became increasingly difficult. But services form an integral part of both manufacturing and sales. For instance, the manufacture of computer software offers a series of services such as training, installation, maintenance etc. and it becomes very complex in segregating the line between goods and services. As a result, manufacturers generally reduce the assessable value of their manufactured goods at low sale prices and claim discounts for post-manufacturing services such as installation and maintenance services.

Such exclusion of services from the manufacturing stage causes difficulties in fixing the manufacturing value of excise duties. Similarly, definitional ambiguities such as erection of something immovable, even though it forms an integral part in production does not fall under excise taxation as the Constitution defines goods as tangible and movable. Moreover, taxation at the manufacturer level tends to distort revenue mobilisation as the profit margins and associated services are not included in the base.

3.8.4 Additional Duties of Excise in Lieu of Sales Tax: Additional duties of excise were basically intended to regulate the commodities of mass consumption at the national level in order to have a uniform tax burden throughout the country as well as controlling the prices of these commodities. Hence, the Central Government placed the idea before the Taxation Enquiry Commission (1953-54). But the Commission rejected the idea outright. In spite of the refusal, the National Developmental Council in 1956, adopted a resolution and recommended replacement of the sales tax on textiles, sugar and tobacco with additional duties of excise despite protests from the state governments. In 1957, Additional Duties of Excise (Goods and Special Importance) Act was enacted and it made provisions for levying additional duties on cotton fabrics, woollen fabrics, rayon or artificial silk fabrics, sugar and tobacco replacing the sales tax levied by the state governments.

Since sales tax on textiles, tobacco and sugar were replaced by the additional duties of excise, these special goods still bear a uniform tax burden throughout the country. Similarly, these commodities bear a uniform taxation throughout the country; they are free from interstate taxation and hence have a free movement across the state borders leading the way for creation of a common market. As the additional duties are collected at the production level itself, scope for evasion is reduced.

Also, as these additional duties are collected along with the basic excise duties with the same procedures, the cost of collection is also low. The revenue collected from additional excise duties are distributed among the states on the basis of the formulae devised by the Finance Commissions. This has acquired the character of a rental arrangement between the Centre and the states. Hence, this can be considered as a first step towards harmonization of taxes in terms of a coordinated common commodity taxation system among the states (horizontal harmonization) and between the centre and the states (vertical harmonization).

A. Core Issues of Additional Duties in Lieu of Sales Tax:

(a) Loss of Fiscal Autonomy of States: The Second Finance Commission, recommended to the Centre, a compensation package to the states to compensate the loss of revenue from the sales tax on these commodities on the basis of the tax rates prevailing in the states and the population of the states. But the trade and the industry encouraged the scheme and urged to cover more commodities. Following the demand, the central government set up a committee under the chairmanship of Mr. B.C. Roy, the then Chief Minister of West Bengal to recommend commodities of mass consumption and special importance. The Committee recommended matches, paper and vegetable products. Later, the Fourth Finance Commission recommended the allocation criteria for disposing the balance amount after the distribution guaranteed amount on the basis of the percentage increase in sales tax revenue collected out of the total sales tax collected in all the states. This was resented by one of the members and he inserted a dissent note stating "reasons of certainty and stability hold well in present case too if anything more clearly than in the distribution of the income tax proceeds". [6]

However, the Fifth Finance Commission recommended that the states can get grants only up to the amount realized in 1956-57 on these commodities and the additional revenue realized would be distributed to the states on the basis of population and the percentage growth of sales tax of states. The states dissatisfied with this recommendation stated that this went against their Constitutional right to have the entire proceeds on the basis of compensation principle. The states further stated that the guaranteed amount based on the sales tax rates prevailing in 1956-57 was not acceptable as the prevailing rate was low in many states.

Further, the Central government has not increased the rates of these commodities for a long time while it increased the basic duties every year. Similarly, the central government is restricting the states from taxing these commodities. Even though there is no legal bar on the states to tax these commodities, there are restrictions as regards the levy of sales tax on these items—since would not receive any share from the proceeds by putting a ceiling of 4 percent on these commodities.

Due to unsatisfactory functioning of the scheme, the National Development Council was convened in December 1970 to deliberate upon the issue.

The Council adopted that except for manufactured tobacco, the remaining commodities would be subjected to ad valorem system of excise duties, the incidence of AED be increased to 10.8 percent of the value of clearances. While fixing the rates for AED items, the central governments should keep a ratio of 2:1 between the yield of basic and special excise duties on the one hand and AED on the other and set up a standing review committee to review the scheme once in a year to make suitable recommendations. But the implementation was not up to the satisfaction of the states.

Even though cotton and man-made fabrics were subjected to ad valorem system, specific duties were continued for sugar, *bidis* and cigarettes.

The setting up of standing review committee was delayed and it was set up only in 1981 and it decided to increase the incidence of additional excise duties, in three stages such as 8.5 percent by 1984-85, 9.7 percent by 1987-88 and 10.8 percent by 1989-90. Only by 1989-90, the incidence had reached the 10.87 percent level—it took almost two decades and keeping in view the financial losses suffered by the states, the states lost their confidence with the Centre. While fixing the rates—the ratio between basic and additional excise duties of 2:1 proposed initially—only in 1982-83, the ratio was attained as 1.79:1. Due to the above reasons, all the states were unhappy with the implementation delays caused by the Centre and made submissions before the Tenth Finance Commission to revoke this rental arrangement and that these commodities be reverted back under the sales taxation of the states.

(b) Extension of the Scheme: During the September 1980 meeting of the National Development Council, it was decided to include vanaspati and life saving drugs under the AED list. Accordingly, in 1981, a committee was set up under the chairmanship of Mr. Mohanlal Sukhadia and later under Mr. Kamalapathi Tripathi to study the extension of this scheme. The Kamalapathi Tripathi Committee recommended in 1983 that vanaspati, life saving drugs and medicines, cement, paper and paper board and petroleum products be included in the AED list and measures should be taken to safeguard the interests of the states in view of the extension of the scheme. But later, it was not implemented, as most states were not happy with the way in which the scheme was implemented in the past and that the Central government was unable to implement the recommendations of the Tripathi Committee.

(c) Amalgamation of Additional Excise Duties with Basic Excise Duties: The amalgamation of AE duties with the basic excise duties were referred to the Ninth Finance Commission by the Central government. But the states expressed dissatisfaction on the basis that it should have been referred to the Ninth Finance Commission only with the agreement of states and the approval of the National Development Council. The states expressed apprehensions that with the amalgamation of AE duties with the basic duties, AE duties will loose its separate identity and their right over the imposition of sales tax would be lost. Further, with the past functioning, the scheme implies that the centre would not be in a position to guarantee the buoyancy of revenue to the states. The Ninth Finance Commission took note of the apprehensions expressed by the states and recommended against the amalgamation of AE duties with basic excise duties.

3.9 Tax Reforms and Excise Duties

As tax policy is an important instrument of economic policy—whenever a new economic policy is introduced, changes in taxation structure should also be brought about. The first and foremost tax reforms committee in India was the Taxation Enquiry Commission of 1953-54 under the chairmanship of Dr. John Mathai. In fact, it laid down the basis for the future expansion in terms of tax rates and commodity coverage and observed that in order to mobilise more revenue, it is necessary to extend excise taxation to items of mass consumption, commonly regarded as essentials in addition to the luxuries at higher tax levels. Major recommendations of the Committee were as under:

1. Extension of excise duty coverage to sewing machines, vegetable oils, woolen textiles, biscuits, paper, electric fans, electric lamps, aerated waters, glasswares, dry batteries, paints, varnishes and ceramics.
2. Proposed significant hikes in the rate of duty on kerosene, sugar, matches, tea and cloth.

The next major set of reforms aimed at the rationalization and simplification of tax structure was the Bhoothlingam Committee in 1967. He made a significant contribution in the case of excise duties by introducing a general excise duty at the rate of 10 percent ad valorem on all manufactured products. Subsequently, the Indirect Taxation Enquiry Committee did the most pioneering study on indirect taxes in 1978 under the chairmanship of Mr. L.K. Jha. The Committee found that the biggest deficiency of the indirect taxation in India was the cascading effects, the multiplicity of rates, specifications, procedure complications, etc. making our taxes complicated, uncertain, discriminatory and administratively difficult. The Committee recommended four tax rates at 10, 20, 30 and 40 percent except for a few products to be taxed at lower or higher rates. A major recommendation of the committee was the introduction of value-added tax at the manufacturing stage (MANVAT) to avoid the cascading effect of input taxation by giving input tax credits for inputs and laid the foundation for the introduction of modified value added tax (MODVAT) in 1986.

The Technical Study Group on Central Excise Tariff Structure (1985) recommended five duty rates; viz. a middle rate representing an average incidence of excise duties, two rates above and below the middle rate and a zero rate. The lower two rates were proposed for inputs and items of mass consumption. The upper rates were proposed for a few inputs and products largely consumed by richer sections of the society. A zero rate was proposed for a few highly essential items. A new scheme called Modified Value Added Tax (MODVAT) was first introduced in 1986. The system permitted the manufacturers to obtain instant and complete reimbursement of excise duty paid on components and raw materials.

3.10 Important Characteristics of MODVAT

3.10.1 Input Credit System: In order to mobilize more financial resources, excise duties were levied on both the final products and the inputs used for manufacturing. Hence, when the output is taxed, inputs too are taxed, resulting in the cascading effect contributing to the higher cost of production and higher tax burden for the consumer. The Indirect Taxation Committee (1978) recommended that the all units of goods may be taxed irrespective of whether the goods are essential or luxury but credit should be given to the inputs. "The twin principles of taxing all units and then relieving from tax those used as inputs, serve to make extended taxation effective while avoiding cascading and distortions" [7] Now, it becomes comprehensive and is universally justified that every producer is taxed for total output of goods and any input that has been taxed can be deductible from excise paid on the final output.

3.10.2 Excise Duty Structure: The main problem associated with the excise tax structure includes the rate of tax, spread, number of tax rates, exemptions and the specific and ad valorem rates. As recommended by the Indirect Taxation Enquiry Committee (1978), the uniform rate of tax should be applied to products falling within a particular category to ensure the uniform incidence of taxation irrespective of consumer's choice. Regarding the number of rates, it recommended four or five basic rates such as 10, 20, 30 and 40 percent and rates more than 40 percent should be fixed only where there is justification for it—for reasons other than more revenue augumentation. [8] The Committee further recommended that the number of rates may be reduced gradually to two or three rates and in case of non-essential commodities tax rates at 30, 40 or 50 percent may be levied and the maximum limit of 50 percent could be extended only in respect of a few items like cigarettes.

3.10.3 Positive Externalities: Under MODVAT, on the environmental side, lower tax rates as well as exemptions may be considered for natural and biological fertilizers and pest retarding agents, which are acting as substitutes for water polluting sources such as chemical fertilizers and pesticides. Under MODVAT, biogas, solar energy and wind energy may be fully exempted. Lower rates of tax for LNG and LPG may also be proposed as these fuels are substitutes against polluting kerosene and firewood and efforts may be made to supply cooking gas to urban and semi-urban areas and promoting bio-gas in rural areas.

3.10.4 Special Excise Duty Rates: For demerit goods such as cigars, cigarettes, chewing tobacco and pan masala and luxury consumer durable goods such as cars, there should be higher rate of tax without any input credit. Motor spirit and diesel and dyes and chemicals may be taxed more as these goods cause damage to the ground water resources.

3.10.5 Import and Exports: All exports are zero-rated and entitled to avail full input credit for the CENVAT paid. Imports should be taxed similar to CENVAT and non-deductible special excise as on domestically produced goods. Since the scheme follows the gross product method, the excise duty paid on inputs used for its production is deducted. It is extended up to the manufacturing level and applies only to basic excise duty and countervailing duty on imports.

While VAT in other countries operates up to retail stage, in India, MODVAT operates only up to the manufacturing level. A study conducted by the National Institute of Public Finance and Policy on the "Operation of MODVAT" shows that industry specific enquiries undertaken by the study team revealed that MODVAT scheme seems to have had a mitigating influence on the cascading effect of multistage excise taxation. [9] Even though no discernible impact on prices of individual commodities covered within MODVAT is known by and large, the scheme does not appear to have caused any adverse effect on their prices. The scheme introduced built-in checks against evasion of excise duty and in general improves the tax compliance.

3.11 MODVAT Administration

3.11.1 Declarative Obligations: MODVAT is, unlike VAT in other countries, a levy on manufactured goods where instant credits are availed on inputs. Every manufacturer of excisable goods is required to register with the Assistant Collector of Central Excise, having jurisdiction over his factory indicating the description of the final products to be manufactured in his factory and revealing the inputs intended to be used in the production of the said final products. In the subsequent period, particularly from April 1, 1994, invoices have been used as a clearance document. Invoices must accompany each consignment transported from factory to other places and should be pre-authenticated by a responsible person of the factory and should be intimated to the Superintendent of Central Excise after the invoices are serially numbered.

The invoices issued by the first and second stage dealers of excisable goods are provided with the MODVAT credit or CENVAT credit. By the 10th of every month, the manufacturer is required to file a monthly return to the Superintendent of Central Excise and pay the CENVAT on a fortnightly basis. Manufacturers of small-scale industries are required to file quarterly returns, indicating the particulars of goods manufactured, cleared and amount of excise duty paid. Also, the particulars of inputs received during the month and the amount of duty taken as credit and information on total duty paid through personal ledger account (PLA) and CENVAT credit should be given along with the details of disposal of inputs and utilization of the credit.

3.11.2 Accounting. Obligations: The manufacturers are given freedom to maintain their accounts regarding receipt, disposal, consumption and inventory of goods containing relevant information. Misuse of MODVAT credit attracts penalties along with interest. The amount of duty payable is recorded in the daily stock account before clearance and the duty is paid monthly either by cash or through CENVAT credit. To check under-invoicing, the Excise Department has additional powers to audit the cost structure of the goods manufactured. The cost audit report would determine the assessable value irrespective of the cost audits done by any law. The cost of undertaking this special audit is borne by the Department.

3.12 Coverage of MODVAT

Initially, the MODVAT was introduced in 1986-87 for selected raw materials used in production of specified goods.

During 1987-88, the coverage was extended to all the commodities except petroleum products, textile products, tobacco, cinematographic films and matches. MODVAT was gradually extended to other commodities. Table 3.6 presents the coverage of MODVAT during the period between 1986-87 and 2003-04.

Table 3.6: Major Changes in the Coverage under MODVAT

Year	Coverage
1986-87	MODVAT introduced for selected raw materials when used in production of specified goods.
1987-88	Most of the raw materials covered under MODVAT.
1988-89	Minor expansion in the coverage of MODVAT.
1989-90	Minor expansion in the coverage of MODVAT.
1990-91	Minor expansion in the coverage of MODVAT.
1991-92	Minor expansion in the coverage of MODVAT.
1992-93	Minor expansion in the coverage of MODVAT.
1993-94	Minor expansion in the coverage of MODVAT.
1994-95	-Capital goods, petroleum products and specified spun yarns covered under MODVAT. -Small-scale industrial (SSI) enterprises given the option to pay normal excise duty in place of concessional duty.
1995-96	-The scheme extended to cut tobacco, plastic woven sacks, specified textiles and equipments. -Scope of SSI concessions enlarged. Turnover limit for availing SSI concessions raised from ₹ 2 crore to ₹ 3 crore. -Conditions of matching raw materials/capital goods with output for allowing MODVAT credit, withdrawn.
1996-97	-MODVAT credit in respect of some capital goods has been denied. -In the case of processed textile fabrics, a deemed MODVAT credit has been allowed, without production of duty paying documents. -The scope of availing MODVAT credit in the case of production of exempt goods supplied to specified buyers such as 100 percent EOUs has been extended. -The rule for reversal of MODVAT credit in respect of exempted final product has been simplified to 20% of value of such goods. -When the manufacturer clears inputs or partially processed inputs for job work, MODVAT credit availed of on this account should be reversed. -MODVAT credit on the basis of invoices issued by third and subsequent dealers denied to check evasion. -In the case of invoices issued by the second stage dealer, credit will be admissible only if the same has been signed by the proper officer. -Mandatory penalty of 100 percent and interest to be charged in case of wrong availment of MODVAT credit on inputs.

1997-98	-Duty rates have been restructured with basic rates of 8, 13 and 18 percent. -Some exemptions have been withdrawn. -Exemption scheme for SSIs has been modified with exclusion of certain goods from its purview. If MODVAT credit is not availed then duty rates are 0, 3 and 5 percent respectively on clearances up to ₹ 30 lakh, next ₹ 20 lakh and next ₹ 50 lakh. -Accumulated MODVAT credit, as on 1.3.1997, with the manufacturers of bulk drugs to lapse. -MODVAT credit allowed to the extent of 75 percent of the CVD paid on goods imported under project imports. -Invoices issued by the depot or consignment agent of an importer made eligible for availing credit.
1998-99	-MODVAT credit in respect of inputs restricted to 95 percent of the excise paid on inputs, with effect from June 2, 1998. -Exemption scheme for SSIs has been liberalised. Duty rates have been modified to 0 and 5 percent respectively on clearances up to ₹ 50 lakh and next ₹ 50 lakh. SSI benefit has been extended to computers while withdrawn on copper alloys. -Maximum retail price (MRP) based assessment has been extended to many products such as chocolates, malt extract, pan masala and glazed tiles.
1999-00	-MODVAT credit in respect of inputs restored to 100 percent. -The restriction on taking MODVAT credit to the extent of 10 percent or the amount of CVD in respect of certain petroleum products has been removed. -The scope of capital goods credit has been extended to duty paid on certain machines. -The exemption in respect of independent processors of yarn has been withdrawn. The duty is fixed at ₹ 5 per kg. with no benefit of MODVAT credit. -The excise duty on packaged tea has been withdrawn. However, on bulk tea, a duty of ₹ 2 per kg. has been imposed. -Eleven existing excise rates have been compressed into three: 8, 16 and 24 percent with two non-rebatable special duty rates: 6 and 16 percent to make up for the existing rates of 30 and 40 percent. -MRP based assessment has been extended to 27 more products. -SSIs have been allowed to pay duty on monthly basis instead of daily. -The discretion to grant ad hoc exemptions has been given up, excepting in the case of goods for security, strategic or charitable purposes.
2000-01	-MODVAT has been renamed as CENVAT with a single. -CENVAT rate of 16 percent. In addition there will be non- rebatable special duty at the rates of 8, 16 or 24 percent. -MODVAT credit extended to all inputs except high speed diesel (HSD) oil and motor spirit (petrol). -MODVAT credit would be available in respect of all finished goods except matches. -MODVAT credit has been extended to all capital goods. -Restriction of 75 percent in respect of capital goods credit on project

	imports has been removed. The condition of installation has been removed. However, availment of capital goods credit has to be spread over two years.
2001-02	-The three special excise duty rates of 8, 16 and 24 percent have been converged into a single rate of 16 percent. As a result, excise duty structure comprises one single rate of 16 percent. -A new levy for National Calamity Contingent Duty has been imposed on cigarettes, *bidis*, pan masala and miscellaneous tobacco products.
2002-03	-Excise duty on LPG, kerosene oil, auto CNG and diesel engines have been raised to 16 from 8 percent. More number of items has been added from the special excise duty rates.
2003-04	-Special excise duty on tyres, aerated soft drinks, polyster filament yarns, air conditioners and components and motor cars have been reduced to 8 from 16 percent.

Source: Budget Documents, Ministry of Finance, Government of India.

3.13 Tax Reforms Committee (1991)

Government of India set up the Tax Reforms Committee (TRC) in 1991 for restructuring and rationalization of direct and indirect tax systems. The Committee headed by Professor Raja J. Chelliah, submitted its report in three installments.

- An interim Report in December 1991
- Final Report Part-I in August 1992.
- Final Report Part-II in January 1993.

In its interim Report, the Committee suggested a series of tax reform measures aimed to improve the revenue buoyancy and simplicity.

Recommendations relating to indirect taxes included the following:

1. Reduction in the number of rates to three (10, 15 and 20 percent), barring the selective excise duty on non-essential commodities or commodities injurious to health which may be taxed at higher rates of 30, 40 and 50 percent.
2. Widening the tax base by taxing services identified by the committee to bring under taxation including advertising, stock broking, automobile insurance and insurance of residential property and jewellery.
3. Valuation procedures should be simplified and specific duties to be replaced by ad valorem duties in respect of most of the goods.

In its final report, the Committee favored the conversion of the present excise system into a genuine value added tax at the manufacturing level spanning over a period of three to four years. It favored the MODVAT credit for all inputs that are used in production and further recommended gradual reduction in the number of rates to three between 10 and 20 percent. It recommended extension of the MODVAT credit for machinery not fully at the time of purchase, but to be provided during a subsequent period. It also recommended the extension of VAT to more important services rendered by productive enterprises. To improve the tax administration, the Committee suggested that the government should not give room for frequent changes and concessions every year, but only structural reforms should be carried out as per the given agenda. Tax collection targets should be fixed realistically by taking into account the growth rates of economy and inflation and it favored for the constitution of a settlement commission for immediate disposal of tax cases. An efficient tax system is a prime requisite to ensure economic efficiency, growth and equity. "Tax reforms since 1991 have helped in correcting structural imbalances in the tax system. They are soft on industry with a view to create new investment climate and make India internationally competitive. By lowering the tax rates, the Government expects speedy industrial development and hence buoyancy in tax revenues". [10]

In September 2002, Government of India constituted two task forces, one for direct and another for indirect taxes under the chairmanship of Dr. Vijay L. Kelkar, advisor to the Minister of Finance and Company Affairs to study the present revenue collection policy and its administration and suggested measures to improve present taxation system aiming at higher tax-to-GDP ratio, focusing on tax structure and tax administration and to improve the export performance and foreign direct investment flows. To rationalize the existing excise system, the Task Force recommended as under:

1. To review the multiple levies such as special duty of excise, cess and additional duty of excise and merge them into single levy of CENVAT.
2. Exemptions for small-scale units whose turnover up to ₹ 1 crore be brought under tax net by 2005-2006 and the exemption ceiling may gradually be brought down to ₹ 50 lakh.
3. Export promotion should be encouraged through special economic zones (SEZs) and export-oriented units (EOUs) only and the present multiplicity of schemes should be dropped. One scheme for allowing free inputs, raw materials for exports and another for duty free capital goods should be evolved and sales in domestic market should be reduced gradually to curb the domestic sales by EOUs and the units in EPZs.

Reforms in Central excise duty emphasizes more on relieving the cascading effect, simplification of assessment rules, procedures and the rationalization of tax rates.

The Task Force on Implementing Fiscal Responsibility and Budget Management Act, 2003 recommended a new levy that is supposed to possess the following characteristics, in order to convert the present CENVAT into a genuine VAT at the Central level.

1. All post-manufacturing services be taxed and the current system of allowing credit on the maximum retail price on goods should be abandoned so as to have a tax base covering all goods and services comprehensively, reaching the final customers.
2. The tax liability should be based on an invoice type credit system in which the credits can be availed on all intermediate goods and services eventually mitigating the influence of cascading during the production and distribution chain.
3. The new levy should be designed on the destination principle leading to the conversion of tax base from

production to consumption in order to cover the imports under taxation and relieve exports from taxation.

4. In order to remove the classification disputes, there should be a minimum number of tax rates. As the present CENVAT tax rate is 16 percent and the services are taxed at 10 percent, a median rate of 12 percent may be fixed for most of the goods and services. In addition, there may be a lower rate of 6 percent on necessities and a higher rate of 20 percent on luxuries items like automobiles, air conditioners, etc.
5. Except for petroleum and tobacco products, all specific rates should be replaced by ad valorem rates which may be set at 6 percent for necessities such as sugar, edible oils and vanaspati and 12 percent for cement.
6. Exemptions may be allowed for a negative list of commodities and services whose consumption should be curbed. Exemptions should also be allowed for all public services, medical services, educational institutions, raw food products, lifesaving drugs and equipments and goods used in national security.
7. Petroleum and tobacco products should be taxed at a higher rate of 20 percent without input credit keeping those commodities under the excise duty.
8. In terms of administrative efficiency and compliance, small dealers with a threshold exemption limit up to ₹ 25 lakh in annual turnover may be exempted from the tax net.
9. A compound rate of 2 percent may be fixed for small dealers whose annual turnover is less than ₹ 40 lakh, and all manufacturers whose annual turnover is above ₹ 40 lakh, should be covered under the integrated goods and service tax.
10. For the purpose of the levy, the owners of the production units defined under the Income Tax Act should be the basic limit unlike manufacturing units and the administration should be based on the audited accounts rather than physical controls.

11. The manufacturer who comes under the tax net is required to register under PAN (permanent account number) and TAN (tax account number) and from his unique identification number, is required to pay his taxes and filing of returns on a monthly basis and those covered under the compound levy are required to do the same on a quarterly basis.
12. A central information system should be set up to verify the transactions and input credits in order to prevent tax evasion and avoidance and all the taxpayers are required to file returns detailing the sales and purchases of goods and services.

Excise duties have increased manifold over the years, rising from 16.8 percent in 1950-51 to around 50 percent during the seventies and early eighties. But, after the introduction of modified value added tax (MODVAT) during 1986-87, its contribution towards the total revenue continues to show a declining trend in terms of GDP and its share has fallen continuously from 4.5 percent in 1980-81, 3.5 percent in 2000-01 and 3.3 percent in 2003-04. The Reserve Bank of India, Annual Bulletin (2002-03) quoted that the tax-GDP ratio of the Central government has suffered a steady deterioration around 10 percent during the nineties and again improved in 2005-06. [11] Since 1986-87, the excise tax revenue has fallen continuously and it is one of the causes for the deteriorating fiscal situation. [12]

3.14 Conclusion

The introduction of MODVAT in 1986 was an important step towards harmonizing excise duty structure in India. It was intended to mitigate cascading input taxation, rationalization of tax rates and simplification of tax procedures to improve efficiency and tax compliance. MODVAT offers instant credits for excise duty paid on components and raw materials. During 2000-01, the scheme was renamed as CENVAT with a single rate of 16 percent. During the post-MODVAT period, a faster rise in MODVAT credits had a dampening effect on net revenue. A faster rise in exports and a declining industrial output affected the gross revenue. Harmonization of excise duty has improved export performance. Further analysis shows that most of the high yielding commodities have exhibited instability in tax revenues. It is strongly recommended that services should be integrated with CENVAT and a lower threshold limit be set up for the small-scale sector. Additional excise duties on sugar, tobacco products and textiles should be allotted to states and merged with the state VATs.

Endnotes

1. Lakdawala, D.T. and Nambiar, K.V. (1972), "Commodity Taxation in India", Sardar Patel Institute of Economics Social Research, Ahmedabad, p. 41.
2. Government of India, "Report of Taxation Enquiry Commission 1953-54", Ministry of Finance, Vol. I, p. 149.
3. Government of India, "Report of the Indirect Taxation Enquiry Committee", Ministry of Finance, Part-II, 1978, p. 17.
4. Sury, M.M. (1988), "Excise Taxation in India", Commonwealth Publications, New Delhi, p. 42.
5. Government of India, "Report of the Indirect Taxation Enquiry Committee", Ministry of Finance, Part-II, 1978, p. 130.
6. Government of India, "Report of Fourth Finance Commission", 1965.
7. Government of India, "Report of the Indirect Taxation Committee", Ministry of Finance, Part-II, p. 17.
8. Government of India, Report of the Indirect Taxation Committee, Ministry of Finance, Part-II, p. 148.
9. Narayana et al. (1991), "The Operation of MODVAT", Sivas Publishing House, New Delhi.
10. Indian Tax Foundation (2003), "Tax Reforms in India 1991-2001", New Delhi, p. 32.
11. "Reserve Bank of India Bulletin, 2002-2003", p. 56.
12. Virmani, Arvind (2002), "Central Value Added Tax (CENVAT)", *International Economic Relations*.

4

Sales Tax

4.1 State Level Sales Tax

Sales tax is a levy on a commodity at one or more points of sale or purchase between the various stages of production and final consumption. Today, it has become a major source of revenue for most of the States comprising 60 to 70 percent of the States' own tax revenues. It dates back to Kautilya's Arthasastra. [1] In the modern times, the erstwhile Bombay Province was the first State in India that levied taxes on sale of tobacco in 1938 by taking advantage of the fiscal autonomy conferred on it by the Government of India Act, 1935. Later, the Central Province introduced it on motor spirit and lubricants in 1939. But Tamil Nadu was the first State in India imposing General Sales Tax in 1939.

The levy of sales tax by the Madras and Central Provinces were challenged by the erstwhile Central government. The Constitutional validity of the Sales Tax on Motor Spirits and Lubricants Taxation Act, 1938 enacted by the legislative assembly of the Central Provinces was questioned in the Supreme Court under Section 213 of the Government of India Act, 1935 on the ground that a union excise duty could be levied between any stage from production to consumption and the sales tax levied by the Provinces was an encroachment of Item 45 of the Central List of the Act, 1935. But these Provinces maintained that the Central excise duty was a levy on production and could be collected immediately on the production of goods irrespective of whether the goods produced are sold or not at the end of production point. The Supreme Court shared this view and upheld the validity of the enactments imposed on sales taxes by these Provinces. This judicial pronouncement clearly demarcated the line between the union excise duty and the sales tax.

Following this, many States introduced sales taxation in their respective States and by 1950, virtually all States had sales tax as one of their sources of revenue following the model of Tamil Nadu. But it was only after the Constitutional Enactment in 1950, which empowered the States to levy taxes on sales, it took a definite shape. [2]

The Constitution Act, 1950, empowered the States to levy "taxes on the sale or purchase of goods other than newspapers" under Entry 54 of List II (State List of the Seventh Schedule). Following the Supreme Court judgment in 1955, the power to impose sales tax was clearly demarcated following the Constitutional Amendment in 1956.

4.1.1 Revenue Significance: Sales taxes have grown substantially over the years as is evident from Table 4.1. It was initially levied as an alternative source of revenue to State excise duties on liquors, as there was a persistent demand for prohibition. But later it has grown into an independent, very elastic and single largest source of revenue for the States in India.

With little less than ₹ 60 crore in 1951-52, it has grown into almost ₹ 5.9 lakh crore in 2015-16, exhibiting a phenomenal growth and buoyancy. Its share in the total tax revenue of States has grown from 15 percent in 1951-52 to 42 percent in 2015-2016. Similarly, its share as a percentage of own tax revenue of States has grown from 26 percent in 1951-52 to almost 64 percent in 2015-2016. Among the indirect taxes of States, its share has grown manifold from 34 percent in 1951-52 to almost 85 percent in 2015-2016. Also, its share in the total revenue of Centre and the States have increased from 10 percent in 1950-51 to about 25.1 percent in 2014-2015 with growing importance as a stable source of revenue to the States. In fact, the State Government's finances would have been in total chaos but for the buoyancy of the sales tax in a situation of inflationary trend.

Over the years, many commodities were added and sales

tax rate revisions were carried out periodically. As the economy grows, sales taxes also grow, as it is more responsive to the changes in the economy with a stable growing demand for consumption. Also, there is a 4 percent tax on inter-State sales laid down by the Central Sales Tax and as a result, there is substantial tax exportation.

Table 4.1: Revenue from Sales Tax in India

Year	Sales Tax Revenue (₹ crore)	Sales Tax as Percent of Total Revenue of States	Sales Tax as Percent of Own Tax Revenue of States	Sales Tax as Percent of Total Indirect Tax Revenue of States
1951-52	59	14.86	25.87	33.96
1961-62	181	16.90	37.51	48.32
1971-72	839	20.77	31.83	58.35
1981-82	4,893	23.17	59.53	66.32
1991-92	21,064	27.10	59.49	66.73
2001-02	76,885	30.00	60.00	70.86
2002-03	86,641	29.50	60.00	70.00
2003-04	98,895	29.58	59.46	69.00
2004-05	1,37,368	50.96	60.00	84.00
2005-06	1,49,313	47.04	61.03	82.14
2006-07	1,62,297	50.96	61.52	82.76
2007-08	1,67,731	47.04	61.56	79.31
2008-09	1,90,817	42.10	60.00	84.05
2009-10	2,31,461	38.94	61.05	88.37
2010-11	2,93,256	40.42	61.57	85.35
2011-12	3,61,332	42.52	62.87	85.42
2012-13	4,22,578	41.79	62.73	84.46
2013-14	5,03,121	43.10	64.94	85.87
2014-15	5,61,597	43.38	64.90	83.88
2015-16	5,94,332	41.92	63.75	84.97

Source: Budget Documents of the State Governments (various years).

4.1.2 Structure of Sales Tax: Since sales taxes are administered by the States, there is no uniformity in structure and administration. Generally, there is a general sales tax (GST) levied on all commodities and a selective sales tax (SST) in which a few selected items alone come under the purview of taxation. Except Assam and West Bengal, all other States have a single Act for imposing GST. In the initial stages of levy of sales tax, the poïnt of levy differed from State to State as all the southern States had multi-point levy. For instance, Gujarat had double point and the remaining States had single point levies. Selective sales tax (SST) is imposed on motor spirit (MST) and purchase tax on selected commodities. Later on, these selective taxes were merged with the GST.

Legally, sales tax is levied on dealers who are either sellers or purchasers. Depending on the nature of commodities, a sales tax or purchase tax is imposed in terms of convenience. Some States like Andhra Pradesh and Kerala have slabs for turnovers and different tax rates are applied to different turnover slabs progressively on dealer's fall under different turnover groups. Even though some States having multi-point or double-point levies, the revenue derived from the first point levy ranges between 60 and 93 percent. [3] Over the years, sales tax has become the most productive and single largest source of revenue for the States. Therefore, more commodities were added and tax rates were increased periodically to generate additional revenues to meet the Plan targets and other contingencies.

4.1.3 Rate of Tax: Generally, the rate of tax is fixed depending on necessity, comfort or luxury of commodities. Necessities are exempted in most of the States or a low rate of 1 to 4 percent is imposed on them. Comforts are taxed between 5 to 10 percent and higher rates from 10 to 20 percent are imposed for luxuries. The tax rate differentiation between the States is one of the most pressing problems of sales tax system as it causing the diversion of trade and shifting manufacturing industries from one State to another. Even within a State, different rates are levied according to the gradations of the same commodity. The range of tax rates lies between 1 and 25 percent. This multiplicity of rates causes confusion and clearly hampers progressivity of the taxes.

Taxation of inputs also differs across the States as some States such as Maharastra and Gujarat tax inputs at 4 percent whereas Madhya Pradesh and Rajasthan tax inputs at a rate of

2 percent and 1 percent respectively. In Delhi however, raw materials are fully exempted. Some States levy surcharges and additional sales taxes to mobilise more revenue to meet the demands of specific projects. For example, Gujarat levies 10 percent surcharge to finance river valley projects. Maharashtra and Punjab also levy at 6 percent surcharge to finance similar projects.

4.1.4 Operation of Sales Tax: The operation of the sales tax starts with the enrolment of traders. The enrolment of traders requires an application in the prescribed form to be submitted to the sales tax officer of the area. The sales tax officer in turn verifies the credentials of the dealer and issues a registration certificate. The registration procedures are not uniform across the States. Without proper verification, there is a possibility for fictitious dealers who in turn practice bill trading leading to the evasion of tax. All the dealers are required to submit monthly, quarterly or annual returns depending on the turnover limits of the dealers. This turnover limits also known as exemption limits that differ across the States.

The sales tax officials carefully scrutinize the returns and the tax paid. The dealers are required to fill a challan in triplicate or quadruplicate for payment of tax and the challan is submitted to the treasury. The original copies are sent to the assessing officers and the third or the fourth copies are submitted to the assessing authorities along with the returns. The annual assessment commences with the submission of all returns within the financial year. The assessing officers scrutinize all the returns and if found correct, accept the returns. Otherwise, the assessing officer issues notices to the dealers calling for records to establish the credentials of the tax particulars furnished in the returns. The assessing authorities are required to examine the records as per the *best judgment assessment.*

Sales tax evasions are rampant in the present existing set up. It is evident not only from the suppression of sales and purchases by the dealers, but also from the corrupt practices adopted by the assessing authorities. Suppression of sales and purchases practiced by the dealers by effecting sales and purchases without bills, same bill being produced for most transactions, destruction of bills without accounting and low-pricing or under invoicing are some of the illegal means of evasion. A major form of evasion is the production of bills showing that the goods in possession are for second sale and such bills look like originals. But on investigation, these transactions are bogus and are effected by the so-called bill traders. Even among the recorded sales and purchases, bogus claims in misclassifying taxable goods as exemptions, bogus claims of purchase of goods from registered dealers who are actually unregistered and claims of second sale are some of the other means of tax evasion.

In inter-State sales too, tax evasion is rampant. Various types of forms are used for goods imported from other States. Some of the dealers make heavy purchases of these forms in short interval of time and disappear without paying any tax. One of the major evasions in inter-State sale is the consignment transfer in which firms are allowed to send their goods to the branches outside the States by producing a special type of form called 'F' forms. By misusing these F-forms (consignment transfers), dealers send their goods of their own States and sell these goods without paying the tax. Similarly, sales tax is evaded on export sales also. As export sales are exempted from tax, dealers using H-forms (H-forms are used for export sales) engage in evasion of tax by collusion with importing and exporting dealers as importing dealers are mostly out of the jurisdiction of the assessing authorities.

4.2 Central Sales Tax

Central sales tax is a levy on inter-State sale or purchase of goods. In federal countries, generally, commodities produced in one state may have to pass through several other states until it reaches for final consumption. Hence, taxation of inter-state trade has a direct impact on the movement of commodities across the state borders as the tax imposed by one state affects consumers in other states. Hence, it becomes necessary to regulate the inter-state trade as well to ensure free flow of goods towards a unified single market. In order to regulate inter-state trade, some basic problems such as what constitute inter-state sales, how to avoid the multiple tax evasion and effecting uniformity in tax laws and tax rates, have to be addressed.

4.2.1 Historical Background: The Constitution Act, 1950, in spite of Article 286 of the Indian Constitution, prohibits the States from levying tax on inter-State sales and import or export sale of goods out of the territory of India. But later in 1953, the Supreme Court in one of its rulings interpreted that if the goods are supplied in a State for sale or purchase for consumption, then such a sale or purchase would be deemed to have taken place within as well as outside the State. As a result, producing States by taking cognizance of the ruling, imposed taxes on inter-State sales and even opened offices in other States too. However, in 1955, the Supreme Court overruled its earlier ruling and held that no State is authorized to impose any levy on inter-State sales, unless or otherwise provided by a law enacted by the Parliament. As per the 1950 Constitution, sales tax was a destination-based consumption tax and the tax has to be levied by the State where the consumption takes place.

However, the Taxation Enquiry Commission (TEC, 1953-54) held a different view that the exporting States should have a minimum share of the inter-State sales tax and recommended for the Constitutional amendments to empower the Union government to impose tax on inter-State sales. However, the TEC, 1953-54 proposed Central legislation for the levy of sales tax on inter-State trade and recommended a rate at which tax should be imposed on sales in the course of inter-State trade and commerce. "As in permitting the levy of sales tax on inter-State trade, the main intention is to ensure that some revenue accrues to exporting States without raising unduly the burden on consumers in the importing State. It further suggested a rate of one percent on all articles except on goods of special importance in inter-State trade". [4] By accepting the recommendations, the Constitutional Amendment (46th Amendment) was enacted in 1956 by the Parliament. It empowers the Parliament:

1. To impose tax on sale or purchase of goods where such sale or purchase takes place in the course of inter-State trade.
2. To evolve basis for determining when a sale or purchase of good takes place outside the State or in the course of import of goods into or export of goods out of territory in India.
3. Any law of a State, in so far as it imposes, or authorizes the imposition of a tax on sale or purchase of goods declared by the Parliament by law to be of special importance in inter-State trade or commerce. The inter- State levy should be subject to such restrictions and conditions in regard to the system of levy, rates and other incidents of the tax, as the Parliament may, by law, specify.

Based on the Sixth Constitutional amendment, the Central Sales Tax (CST) Act, 1956 was passed in the Parliament and a levy at the rate of 1 percent on the inter-State sale of goods was fixed. The CST Act, 1956, provided the basis for eliminating illegal inter-State evasion of purchases made outside the States, a degree of uniformity on the maximum rate of sales taxation on particular raw materials of importance in the country and some sales tax revenue to the exporting States.

4.2.2 Rationale: If there were no tax on inter-State sales, inter-State trade volume would be more and the consumers would be left with an option of buying cheap goods produced in other States. As a result, local manufacturers and traders would be subjected to a disadvantaged position as compared with the manufacturers and traders outside the States. Hence, in the absence of a levy on inter-State trade, it would keep local businesses at a disadvantaged position. If the producing and consuming States would tax at their usual rates, the tax burden would be unduly huge for consumers.

Hence, taxation fulfils the objectives of taxing commodities that do not bear heavier burden than the local products and hereby the local products are not discriminated against the imported substitutes. Following these objectives, the CST Act provides two different rates of tax. A lower rate of 4 percent on inter-State trade to registered dealers by documenting transactions through the use of C-forms as the commodity is taxed by the importing State as well. Such C-forms are issued in importing State by the importing registered dealers within that State to avail the concessional rate of tax. Another rate of 10 percent is levied for inter-State sales on unregistered dealers, as the unregistered dealers pay no tax to the State exchequer as well as it discourages them from purchasing from other States for any competitive advantage. Even though the basic intentions of the CST Act is good but the burden of bearing this rate as well as the usual tax rates of the importing States was unduly heavy.

Due to this heavy burden, local consumers are forced to buy the locally produced goods, discouraging the development of a national common market. In case of certain commodities, produced only in few States, the CST imposes a higher burden on consumers of importing States, resulting in the discrimination between consumers of different States.

4.2.3 Revenue Importance: Initially, inter-State sale of goods was taxed at the rate of 1 percent by the exporting State and this rate was applicable only for the registered dealers. The rate of Central sales tax was raised from 1 percent to 2 percent in 1963. Again in 1966, CST was raised from 2 percent to 3 percent. In 1975, in order to mobilize more revenue for the States, this rate was raised to 4 percent. While raising the CST rate from 3 percent to 4 percent in 1975, most of the consuming States opposed the hike as the incidence of CST fell on the consumers in the importing States, and any further hike would have seriously impaired the revenue generating capacity of these States. Further, increase in tax rates would have an adverse effect on the prices of goods. From Table 4.2, it is apparent that the inter-State taxation (CST) leads to inter-regional inequity. [5]

Table 4.2: CST Revenue Share (2014-2015)

S. No.	States	CST (₹ crore)	GSDP (₹ crore)	Population Share (%)	GSDP Share (%)	CST Share
1.	Gujarat	5,489	4,52,625	4.99	15.4	7.7
2.	Maharashtra	4,647	9,47,550	9.29	13.0	16.1
3.	Tamil Nadu	3,439	5,15,458	5.96	9.6	8.8
4.	Uttar Pradesh	3,421	4,92,384	16.49	9.6	8.4
5.	West Bengal	2,204	3,98,387	7.55	6.2	6.8
6.	NCT Delhi	2,151	2,38,026	1.38	6.0	4.1
7.	Haryana	1,963	2,15,146	2.09	5.5	3.7
8.	Andhra Pradesh	1,825	4,81,953	7.00	5.1	8.2
9.	Chhattisgarh	1,609	1,00,842	2.11	4.5	1.7
10.	Rajasthan	1,595	2,72,227	5.67	4.5	4.6
11.	Karnataka	1,500	3,44,106	5.05	4.2	5.9
12.	Jharkhand	1,269	1,18,743	2.72	3.5	2.0
13.	Madhya Pradesh	1,000	2,53,533	6.00	2.8	4.3
14.	Odisha	919	1,48,576	3.47	2.6	2.5
15.	Assam	718	92,432	2.58	2.0	1.6
16.	Punjab	567	1,83,298	2.29	1.6	3.1
17.	Kerala	459	2,26,208	2.76	1.3	3.9
18.	Uttarakhand	450	77,552	0.84	1.3	1.3
19.	Himachal Pradesh	290	47,255	0.57	0.8	0.8
20.	Goa	160	30,345	0.12	0.4	0.5
21.	Bihar	75	1,89,789	8.58	0.2	3.2
22.	Jammu & Kashmir	0	45,126	1.04	0.0	0.8

Sources: (a) State Budget Documents; (b) National Accounts Statistics.

The top five high income States with a population share of 19 percent, generated 30.5 percent of gross state domestic product (GSDP) and with a 25.4 percent share in the total household consumption, accounted for 38.6 percent share in inter-State sales tax revenue during 2002-2003. On the other hand, low-income States with a population share of 41.2 percent, generated 27.8 percent share in GSDP and having 34 percent share in total household consumption, accounted for just 20 percent share in the CST paid. Among the States, only six States, viz. Maharastra (16.82), Gujarat (9.9), Haryana (8.72), Tamil Nadu (8.95), Karnataka (6.99) and Andhra Pradesh (7.68), had a 60 percent share in CST revenue.

Hence, through CST, tax burden was exported from rich producing States to the consumers in the importing States. The Indirect Taxation Enquiry Committee (1978) looked into this problem and ascertained that the sole objective of setting a lower tax rate of 1 percent was to ensure that there should not be any undue burden on the consumers in the importing States; at the same time some revenue also accrues to the producing States. But due to higher CST, the objective of levying CST has failed and it has become an instrument of transferring the resources from the less developed States to the better-developed States.

4.2.4 Tax Exportation: Also the tax burden exported from better developed States to the less developed States contains the CST collected as well as the embedded input taxes imposed in the producing States. A conservative estimate of tax exportation is attempted in Table 4.3, based on the National Sample Survey (NSS-2011).

4.2.5 Impact of CST: Due to the imposition of 4 percent tax on inter-State sales, many manufacturers consign their products to their depots in other States without attracting the CST. This puts the small traders at a disadvantage, as they do not have the means to set up depots in other States. Due to these reasons, the TRC recommended the reversion of the tax rate to 1 percent as originally fixed. The Committee further added that reversion of tax rate to 1 percent would lead to rationalization of input taxation. Even if sale tax on inputs were higher than the CST rate, the manufacturers import inputs from other States by paying a lower rate of 1 percent tax.

The loss of revenue will be compensated as dealers may not resort to consignment transfers and pay the tax by taking advantage of the lower tax rate. Similarly, even if the CST revenue decreases, the capacity of the States to levy sales tax on goods originating outside the State would improve. The CST Act, 1956 prohibits the States to fix the rebate of tax at not more than 4 percent, and cannot be levied more than once within the State. Further, it introduced the provision of declared goods.

The TEC is of the view that a minimum number of commodities having an inter-State bearing should be exempted from inter-State sales. According to the recommendation of the TEC, coal, iron and steel, cotton, hides and skins, oilseeds and jute were added to the list of declared goods. Later, cotton yarn was included in 1957. In 1976, certain specified pulses, cereals and crude oil were added to the list.

Table 4.3: Tax Exportation (2014-15)

(₹ crore)

States	Total Household Consumption	Percent of Total Consumption	Total Sales Tax Collections	Percent of Total Sales Tax Collection
1	2	3	4	5
Gujarat	4,66,209	9.5	32,214	6.1
Tamil Nadu	5,34,993	10.0	34,072	7.0
Andhra Pradesh	5,80,850	9.6	36,362	7.6
Haryana	1,98,712	5.3	19,302	2.6
Karnataka	3,97,424	7.1	26,759	5.2
NCT Delhi	2,13,997	4.3	15,137	2.8
Maharashtra	8,78,918	11.8	42,445	11.5
Kerala	3,43,924	5.0	19,581	4.5
Punjab	2,44,568	3.6	13,716	3.2
Goa	15,286	0.5	1,780	0.2
Chhattisgarh	1,37,570	1.8	5,481	1.8
Odisha	1,91,069	2.5	9,059	2.5
Jammu & Kashmir	99,356	1.0	3,982	1.3
Jharkhand	1,45,212	1.7	5,464	1.9
Himachal Pradesh	1,37,570	1.1	3,985	1.8
Uttarkhand	1,37,570	1.0	3,716	1.8
Assam	1,75,784	1.5	5,167	2.3
Madhya Pradesh	2,82,782	3.1	24,859	3.7
Rajasthan	4,05,066	4.6	16,938	5.3
Bihar	4,20,352	1.9	7,307	5.5
West Bengal	5,88,493	5.1	17,946	7.7
Uttar Pradesh	10,54,701	8.1	28,993	13.8
Total	76,42,763	100		100

Contd...

States	Difference	Effective Tax Rate (4/2) x 100	Tax Exported (6) x (4)
1	6	7	8
Gujarat	3.4	8.1	1,282
Tamil Nadu	3.0	7.4	1,195
Andhra Pradesh	2.0	6.6	764
Haryana	2.7	10.7	574
Karnataka	1.9	7.1	537
NCT Delhi	1.5	8.1	259
Maharashtra	0.3	5.4	141
Kerala	0.5	5.8	100
Punjab	0.4	5.8	57
Goa	0.3	12.7	6
Chhattisgarh	0.0	5.2	0
Odisha	0.0	5.2	0
Jammu & Kashmir	-0.3	4.0	-12
Jharkhand	-0.2	4.6	-13
Himachal Pradesh	-0.7	3.1	-30
Uttarkhand	-0.8	3.0	-33
Assam	-0.8	3.3	-47
Madhya Pradesh	-0.6	4.4	-75
Rajasthan	-0.7	4.6	-130
Bihar	-3.6	1.8	-266
West Bengal	-2.6	3.4	-524
Uttar Pradesh	-5.7	3.1	-1848
Total	0	5.2	

Sources: (i) Consumer Expenditure (2011) from National Sample Survey Organization; (ii) Sales Tax Collections, Indian Public Finance Statistics.

In the subsequent years, the rate of tax for these declared goods was fixed at 4 percent with the exemption of oilseeds and cotton yarn, taxable at 2 percent. In 1981, during the meeting of Chief Ministers, refined oil, life saving drugs and kerosene were recommended to be included in the list of declared goods. But it was not implemented as the Kamalapathi Tripathi Committee appointed by the government added more commodities such as cement, medicines, paper and paper products and petroleum products that were not acceptable to the States. As the Constitution empowers the State government to levy tax on goods only, excluding services, the hoteliers and works contractors evade taxes on a large scale.

Further, evasion from consignment transfers without paying inter-State sales tax has become a serious problem for many State governments. The Central government on insistence by the States, accepted the proposal for amending the Constitution to empower the States to levy taxes on consignment transfers, works contract and hotel services. But the Indirect Taxation Enquiry Committee differed with the government that taxing of services should be retained with the Central government. The Central government amended the Constitution on the recommended provisions, leaving out consignment transfers and sale of services.

C-forms are issued to the registered dealers in the importing States who in turn submit the same to the exporting dealers to avail the concessional 4 percent rate of tax if the goods are taxed not less than 4 percent in the exporting State. The CST on unregistered dealers if the good is not a declared one would attract a tax rate of 10 percent or a higher rate applicable in the exporting State. But, these unregistered dealers are ready to pay the tax if the rate applicable in the State is lower than 10 percent. Sale of declared goods to the unregistered dealers outside the State attracts twice the rate applicable within the State.

However, the enforcement is very difficult in case, the unregistered dealer happens to be a local dealer who pays not more than 4 percent only at the local rate. Suppose that the rate of tax on the sale of a good is less than 4 percent and if such goods are exported to another State, there is no need to use C-form. Such transactions would result in the loss of revenue for the importing States; as such transactions would go unrecorded in the absence of C-forms. The misuse of C-forms for inter-state sales and F-forms for consignment transfers leads to large scale evasion through fake forms as the States print these forms through private printers.

A tax on inter-State sales would fall on all commodities including inputs. If no set off is given in the succeeding transactions then the rate of tax on goods produced in another

State would be higher than the good itself made within the State. Such goods with embedded taxes would largely impair the competitiveness in the global market.

To trace the volume of inter-State trade, check posts have been erected across the borders. These border check posts have become centres of corruption, causing huge traffic jams and have acted as a barrier to the free flow of commodities. A commodity, which has been imported for consumption from another State, would be subjected to the local sales tax in addition to the CST which it already bears. As a result, burden of taxes is shifted to the consumer in the importing States. Hence, there will be encouragement for producing such commodities locally. Ultimately, the exporting State faces a stiff competition from other States and will loose a substantial loss in production of the commodity concerned. In other words, CST works like a tax on imports levied to protect domestic industry and introduces potential distortions in the decision-making in both the exporting and the importing States. [6]

When a good passes through various stages of production without any set off, the tax at every stage is a tax on taxes earlier paid, leading to cascading. Large producers have opened stock yards in various States and in the name of consignment transfers, transfer goods to these stock yards to avoid CST. This problem has been pointed out by the producing States and has been appraised to the Central government with a view to bring the consignment transfer under the purview of inter-State sales. The Constitution was amended (46th Amendment) subsequently but no act was enacted since no agreement was reached among the States on the rate of tax to be levied on these transfers—a solution to this problem has been eluding for more than a decade.

4.2.6 Reforming CST: The Indirect Taxation Enquiry Committee (1977) recommended, "the important step to be taken towards rationalization of sales tax system is to bring about a reduction in the rate of CST from the existing 4 percent level to 1 percent by stages if necessary. Such a low rate of tax on inter-State sales while serving as a means of preventing large scale evasion of tax on internal sales would go a long way towards preventing the export of taxation levied by one State to the residents of other States". [7] The Tax Reforms Committee (1991) in its report stated that tax on consignment transfers along with in the central sales tax at a rate 4 percent would lead to inefficient resource allocation and loss of welfare as the 4 percent CST along with consignment tax acts as a barrier to the development of a unified common market. [8] Fragmentation of common markets fails to capitalise the economies to scale inherent in large common markets and goes against the integration of Indian economy with rest of the world. Further, the TRC felt that the Central Government has a commitment in giving effect to the 46th Constitutional amendment of taxing consignment transfers. It suggested the following ways to reduce the ill effects of CST and consignment tax.

1. Importing States has to give credit for the sales tax payable to the exporting States.
2. In turn, exporting States credit the same to a central pool and the total collections of these two taxes would be shared among the States according to an agreed formula.
3. The rate of CST and consignment tax would be 2 percent.

Only if there is a broad agreement among the States regarding the reduction of CST to 1 percent, the Central government can enact a law to impose tax on consignment transfers, revert back the power to levy sales tax on sugar, textiles and tobacco, abolish the entry taxes in municipal areas and eliminate the cascading effects of sales tax on inputs. If the compromise formula worked out between States and Centre succeeds, it will herald a new era in the taxation history of the country.

The main aim of any taxation system should be reducing the prices of goods and improving their competitiveness in the global market, minimizing the cost of production by mitigating the cascading effect, avoiding distortions in production and consumption and eliminating harmful exportation in inter-State trade with higher tax compliance. In such a system, taxation of inter-State trade is helpful in achieving an ideal tax system.

The study team of National Institute of Public Finance and Policy (NIPFP, 1994) opined that the inter-State sales taxation in India is a major distortion factor in the operation of the Indian economy and concluded that though inter-State sales taxation was introduced as an instrument to regulate such sales across the States, its operation has impeded growth and diminished welfare by acting as a barrier to free trade and specialization within the country and that it has given rise to problems such as tax cascading, tax exportation and tax competition and tax evasion. Further, it added that for achieving a unified national common market, it is imperative to remove the inter-State sales tax so as to relieve all hidden taxes on exports and to minimize distortions in the location of industries. Unless the taxation system is radically reformed, there is a potential threat for the Indian companies from more intense competition from open economies around Asia. [9]

Removing CST is a major problem since revenue from CST has a relative share of 16 percent among sales tax revenues. As 60 percent of the CST revenue is being collected by only six States, these States will face fiscal imbalances, as a result of sudden removal of CST. A suitable compensation package has to be worked out from alternative sources for the anticipated loss of revenue for these States in the event of removing CST. As already mentioned, sudden removal of CST would mean a substantial loss for the major producing States, a gradual reduction of CST rate from 4 percent to 0 is the most feasible solution.

Reduction of CST from 4 percent to 3 percent means a loss of CST revenue to the tune of 25 percent. But the actual loss would be less than 25 percent since most of the commodities in several States bear less than a 3 percent CST rate. If the States want to reduce the rates to boost inter-State trade, the local sales tax rates should be less than 4 percent.

Rao (2003), [10] worked out a conservative estimate for the State of Karnataka for reducing the CST rate from 4 percent to 2 percent. He estimated that the consignment transfers roughly constitute 60 percent of the inter-State sales and the reduction of CST rate from 4 percent to 2 percent would improve the tax base by 30 percent and that 50 percent of the consignment sales would transform into inter-State sales. This would mean that the tax base would be increased to 130 percent, the tax rate reduced from 4 to 2 percent, the CST revenue would be 65 percent and the expected loss would be 35 percent. But consignment transfers would be more in better industrialized State such as Maharastra and Gujarat where export of finished goods is more than the primary goods and raw materials and in such higher levels of value-added and mark-up situation, dealers would derive better trade margins.

On the other hand, if there is a set off mechanism for the inputs, there will be a reduction in the consignment transfers. For states such as Andhra Pradesh, Haryana and Punjab, where the majority of exports constitute agricultural products, a major part of the consignment transfer will come under the purview of the CST. In the mineral exporting states such as Madhya Pradesh, Jharkhand, Odisha and Chattisgarh, there will be an improvement in the inter-State sales from consignment transfers as the freight equalization scheme favours inter-State sale rather than consignment transfer.

Hence, inter-State sales would be more in future, as and when there is a reduction in the rate of CST. In the long run, when CST is phased out, it is expected that the tax base of the sales taxes would be expanded which in turn would trigger improved efficiency and rapid economic development. Apparently, phasing out CST in the long run would remove all the impediments to the free movement of goods and achieve a unified large common market resulting in an increased efficiency and growth.

But, in the short run, all inter-State sales should be recorded by making C-form compulsory. What is required for the future is that VAT is implemented in identifying the genuine dealers who are exporting goods to another State to become eligible for refund of input taxes. In case of declared goods, an amendment is needed to tax more than once in order to have a comprehensive VAT. The three commodities such as sugar, tobacco and textiles should be freed both from the (AEDILST) additional excise duties. In the long run, zero-rating of CST will result in the removal of barriers to free trade and achieve a large unified common market.

4.3 Overall Weaknesses of the Present System

4.3.1 Point of Levy: In India, most of the States initially followed either the multipoint levy of the Madras system or the retail point levy of the Bengal system. But in due course of time, administrative difficulties arose with the retail point system. With too many dealers, many States opted for the single point levy, including Tamil Nadu, which is the origin for the multipoint levy system. Gujarat has three points of levy with high yielding commodities under the first point, low yielding with the last point and demerit goods under both first and last points. The main advantage of multipoint levy is the reduced scope for tax evasion as it gives enough opportunity to check the accounts at each stage and with the low rate of tax, there is less incentive for evasion.

On the other hand, it has not found favour with the tax administrators as it involves heavy workload with too many assessees and the chance for illegal suppression of sales at the intermediate stages. In the case of double point levy, it is easy to administer but there is ample opportunity for evasion at the last point. But, single point levy is the most favoured one as its administration is simple with a smaller number of assessees who are either manufacturers or wholesalers.

However, it fails to capture the value added at the successive stages with a substantial loss of revenue. Although, last point levy captures value added at each stage, it is difficult to administer with too many assessees and there is a large scope for evasion. By studying all the options, the Indirect Taxation Enquiry Committee (1978) favoured the single point levy at the last stage and provided opportunities for the State governments to determine the kind of burden that should be imposed on the consumers of different products. [11]

In spite of this, most States adopted the single point levy at the first stage and derived the maximum revenue at this point. In order to mobilize more and more revenue to meet the ever-increasing social obligations, most States imposed levies in the form of surcharges, additional sales taxes and turnover taxes, etc. The turnover tax is mostly a multipoint levy that is levied on the gross turnover of dealers with turnovers in excess of the exemption threshold and applied to intermediate dealers as well.

The above changes were effected through various legislations and hereby dealers are required to file as many returns every year and assessments have to be made separately for each of them resulting in the huge backlog of pending assessments and piling up of arrears. With a narrow base and in order to mobilise a given target of revenue, taxes at the first point are levied at high rates that in turn stimulates the business houses to look for ways to avoid tax and lobby for concessions and exemptions. Also, in the first point sales taxation, business firms try to avoid taxes by making sales to its sister concerns at a relatively low prices and by moving certain services beyond the first point.

A study done by NIPFP (1994) in Andhra Pradesh shows that even with all these tax evasions, the trade margin between first and second sales was found to be as high as 100 percent and the difference between the first and second sale price varied between 4 percent and 300 percent in the case of consumer durables. Even under the single point taxation, intermediate dealers too are required to enrol and file returns so as to avail exemptions since the registered dealers have already paid the tax. But in practice, a large number of invoices are false and there is a possibility of bill trading.

Registered dealers sell goods purchased from both within and outside the States and under the first point taxation, those dealers are required to tax the imports in their selling prices. But, in practice, the goods purchased within the State too can be resold without any tax, as many dealers do not familiarize with the dual complex inventory procedures.

Hence, all State governments have to trace the inter-State purchases and erect check posts at their borders. In the first point sale, the sale may be effected to a manufacturer or the wholesaler, or to a retailer but in effect, the prices would be different. Hence, the effective tax rate defined as the ratio of tax to the final consumer price may not be uniform due to differences in the magnitude of value additions at each trade level. As a result, the effective tax rates not only vary across products but also across different dealers. This lack of neutrality creates distortions in production, consumption and inequities among the competing firms which force even the honest dealers to resort to activities unethical and against law. [12]

4.3.2 Cascading Input Taxation: Constrained with the narrow base and exclusion of services, States levied taxes on all inputs, capital and intermediate goods. The cost of production increases as the producers and middlemen require huge amount of working capital to maintain necessary stock of inputs. The prices of the finished goods tend to reflect the sales taxes imposed on the inputs used.

In addition, the middlemen too apply mark-ups to purchase prices and the mark-ups will be applicable to the tax component of the purchase price as well. In other words, general prices are raised many times more than the amount of tax, accentuating the forces of inflation in general and cost-push inflation in particular. The Taxation Enquiry Commission (1953) observed, "Between 1938-39 and 1953-54, the price level increased four-fold while the increase in revenue due to the rate increase was only 1.25 percent.

The cascading incidence under input taxation can be better perceived from Table 4.4.

Table 4.4: Cascading Incidence under Input Taxation

Dealer	Cost of Inputs	Price Before Tax	Tax @ 10 Percent	Sale Price With Tax	Value Added
X	0	100	10	110	100
Y	110	170	17	187	60
Z	187	250	25	275	63
	Total		52		223

Difference between the final selling price and cost = 275-187 = 88
Tax on value added @ 10 percent of 223 = 22.3
Therefore, cascading due to tax on inputs = 52-22.3 = 29.70
Additional cascading caused by price mark-up on tax = 88-52 = 36.

In cascading sales tax system, large vertically integrated companies gain at the expense of small companies. For example, in the production of cloth, the tax is levied initially on the value of cotton purchased, next on the value of yarn manufactured and finally on the value of cloth manufactured. This leads to vertical integration as the single firm which performs all the three activities itself has to pay tax only on the value of manufactured cloth and sells the cloth at a lower price which further leads to economies of scale and monopoly power. Further, input taxation puts the imported goods at a relatively advantageous position than the goods manufactured at home and the amount of tax paid on indigenously produced goods exceeds that paid on a similar imported commodity thereby making the imported goods cheaper than the goods produced at home.

Some States allow input tax credits for raw materials used in the manufacture of taxable goods sold within the State and others levy a tax on inputs varying between 2 to 4 percent. It has been estimated that the taxes on inputs had a 30 percent share in the overall sales tax collections of the States and from the economic point of view, it is injurious to the economy as it increased the cost of production and paved the way for lobbying for tax concessions to start new industries. In order to remove this cascading system of input taxation, it is highly essential to completely set off on all inputs which have been paid earlier in order to improve the competitiveness of goods manufactured in India, in the global market. Table 4.5 reveals the sales tax rate on inputs.

4.3.3 Multiplicity of Tax Rates: Under the single point taxation system, a narrow base consists of first sellers, usually the manufacturers or wholesalers or importers. Under the system, the State governments impose high rates of taxes in order to mobilise the targeted revenue. At the same time, some tax concessions in the form of reduced tax rates are also given on essentials.

Table 4.5: Sales Tax Rate on Inputs (2003-04)

State	**Basic Rate** (in percentage)
Andhra Pradesh	4
Bihar	3
Delhi	0
Goa	0
Gujarat	set off on purchase
Haryana	0
Himachal Pradesh	1
Karnataka	4
Kerala	2.5
Madhya Pradesh	4
Maharashtra	4
Manipur	0
Odisha	4
Punjab	0
Rajasthan	0 to 3
Tamil Nadu	3
Uttar Pradesh	0 to 4
West Bengal	2

Source: Office of Commissioners of Commercial Taxes of the States.

However, in the name of rate differentiation among commodities, every State has a plethora of rates, which are frequently altered depending on various reasons. Such innumerable rates often lead to confusion and legally challenged in highest courts for adjudication on whether a particular commodity belongs to a particular category or not for the purpose of sales taxation. Similarly, turnover taxes levied as supplements to sales tax too lead to a multiple number of rates as different rates are applied to the different sizes of turnovers. Moreover, if there are surcharges, then the number of rates can increase further. In Andhra Pradesh, sales tax is charged along with the surcharge and the turnover, resulting in more than 100 rates of taxes on different ranges of turnover sizes. [13] Table 4.6 presents the multiplicity of tax rates prevailing in the different States.

Very often, some of the States change their tax rates in view of tax competition from other States in order to attract more investments and some States resort to additional levies, surcharges, etc. so as to make the system totally non-transparent with arbitrary and unpredictable tax incidence.

4.3.4 Lack of Uniformity in the Structure of Sales Tax: Lack of uniformity in the structure of sales taxes in different States is one of the most pressing problems of sales taxation in India. Generally, different sales tax rates are levied on commodities depending on whether the commodity is an essential, durable, comfort or a luxury one. Essentials such as food items comprising cereals and pulses are fully exempt in some States and in the remaining States they are taxed at low rates ranging from 1 to 4 percent. Durables or comforts are usually taxed moderately between 5 to 12 percent and the luxuries are taxed at higher rates between 15 to 25 percent. But these tax rates vary among the States and create unhealthy tax competition between the States. This inter-State tax competition not only leads to trade diversions but also creates distortions in consumption and production.

The Committee of Finance Minister on Sales Tax Reform (1995), remarked that the inter-State trade war between the States leads to the unwisely low taxation of luxuries such as motor cars being taxed at 3.5 percent and food grains being taxed at 4 percent in Punjab, bicycles being taxed at a rate more than the motor cars in five out of seventeen States and medicines being taxed at higher rates than the motor cars in nine out of seventeen States. [14]

Table 4.6: Multiplicity of Tax Rates

S. No.	State	Minimum Rate	Maximum Rate	No. of Rates
1.	Andhra Pradesh	0	20	10
2.	Assam	0	20	6
3.	Delhi	0	20	7
4.	Gujarat	0	22	12
5.	Haryana	0	20	9
6.	Jammu & Kashmir	1	30	8
7.	Karnataka	0	20	11
8.	Kerala	1	30	13
9.	Madhya Pradesh	0	25	8
10.	Maharashtra	0	23	14
11.	Meghalaya	0	25	7
12.	Nagaland	0	20	6
13.	Rajasthan	0	22	12
14.	Sikkim	0	20	7
15.	Himachal Pradesh	0	15	11
16.	Odisha	0	20	11
17.	Punjab	0	20	11
18.	Tamil Nadu	0	30	14
19.	Tripura	0	20	13
20.	Uttar Pradesh	0	32	15
21.	West Bengal	0	20	15

Source: Office of Commissioners of Sales and Commercial Taxes of the States.

On similar rate variations, the Committee further pointed out there were wide variations in the absence of harmonization as motor cars were taxed from 3 percent in Goa to 12 percent in Bihar. Karnataka levies leather goods at a high rate of 23 percent whereas in Maharastra, it is fully exempted. Similarly, plastic goods carry a rate of 5 percent in Tamil Nadu and 12 percent in Madhya Pradesh, Orissa and Punjab. [15] Hence, there is a need for tax harmonization of sales tax rates in India so as to ensure uniformity.

In an attempt to discuss the issues and suggest measures, four regional councils were set up to take an important step in the right direction. Even though these councils deliberated the various issues of tax harmonization, it did not yield the desired results as the composition of taxable goods differed between the States and the need to provide tax incentives to attract more industries and investment. However, it was strongly felt that the prevailing low rates in Union Territories on high value goods (motor cars) should be increased in consonance with the floor rate in the nearby State.

The Indirect Taxation Enquiry Committee (1978), [16] attached much importance on the role of regional councils in deliberating matters concerning the inter-State harmonization and policy co-ordination. But only in 1993, the then Union Finance Minister entrusted the issue of uniform sales tax to the National Institute of Public Finance and Policy (NIPFP) to suggest measures and action programs pertaining to the reform of sales tax. The NIPFP submitted the report to the Committee of State Finance Ministers for further deliberation.

The Committee recommended four general floor rate categories (1 and 20) and barring the States from fixing any rate below the floor rate in each category. These issues were discussed subsequently in a series of meetings held on behalf of successive Union Finance Ministers and suggested three floor rates: 0 percent, 4 percent and a standard rate of 12.5 percent including a higher rate of 20 percent for liquor.

4.3.5 Exemptions: Exemption in sales taxes is offered to relieve the tax burden on certain commodities, which are consumed mostly by the poorest sections of the society or as an incentive to industry. Many State governments offer variety of exemptions to attract more industries in the form of tax holidays and deferrals. As the tax competition hots up between the States, the tax bases of the States are seriously eroded, resulting in revenue loss. The estimated loss is supposed to be in the range of 15 percent to 20 percent.

However, Purohit (1975), [17] made an economic analysis of these exemptions and pointed out that from the point of view of equity and administrative expediency, some of these exempted commodities may be taxed. The Committee of State Finance Ministers on Sales Tax Reform pointed out that the incentives offered by some State governments results in the revenue loss to those States with no tangible gain in investments and recommended the abolition of these tax incentives for industrial development in backward areas from April 1, 1997. [18]

For promoting village industries, handicrafts and handmade goods, tax exemptions are essential. Similarly, exemptions should be applied to items that have social implications such as natural and unprocessed products, books and bicycles. Table 4.7 presents the tax incentives in terms of deferrals and tax holidays during the period.

4.3.6 Lack of Uniformity in Tax Administration: Tax administration procedures differ from State to State and there is no uniformity even in the definitions of year, assessment, dealer, turnover limit, registration procedure, etc. Hence, manufacturers and dealers of bigger companies having factories and godowns in different parts of the country have to face great hardship and difficulty in familiarizing with the different tax laws in various States.

Hence, the Taxation Enquiry Commission (1953-54), directed the Central government to draft a model sales tax law to be adopted by the States with slight modifications according to the needs of the States. So far, no steps have been taken in this direction and even the Committee of State Finance Ministers did not make any specific recommendation to evolve uniform procedures in tax administration.

Table 4.7: States Incentives as in 1993

S. No.	State	Deferrals (years)	Tax (years)	Tax Applicable to Sale/Inputs
1.	Andhra Pradesh	10	5	Sale
2.	Assam	-	7	Sale and Inputs
3.	Bihar	5	5	Output
4.	Gujarat	6-9	6-9	Sale
5.	Haryana	5-9	5-9	Sale
6.	Himachal Pradesh	6-12	4-12	Sale
7.	Jammu & Kashmir	10	10	Sale and Inputs
8.	Karnataka	6-8	4-7	Sale
9.	Goa	12-15	12-15	Sale
10.	Kerala	6-10	4-7	Sale
11.	Madhya Pradesh	2-11	2-11	Sale and Inputs
12.	Maharashtra	3-10	3-10	Sale and Inputs
13.	Meghalaya	5	5	Sale and Inputs
14.	Orissa	5	7	Sale and Inputs
15.	Punjab	-	7-10	Sale and Inputs
16.	Rajasthan	7-11	7-11	Sale and Inputs
17.	Tamil Nadu	10-14	5-7	Sale and Inputs
18.	Tripura	-	5	Sale and Inputs
19.	Uttar Pradesh	8-10	8-10	Sale and Inputs
20.	West Bengal	5-10	4-90	Inputs

Source: Chamber of Commerce and Industry, September 1993.

As the exemption limits vary from State to State, the number of dealers under tax net also differs. Hence, the current taxable limits may be made uniform and rationalized. As the current system of verification of documents for establishing the bonafides of the dealers is faulty, the current system is more prone to registration of bogus dealers. As the existing system does not require the dealers to file their books of accounts at the end of each year, bogus dealers manipulate accounts and submit the same to the assessing authorities at a later date.

4.4 Conclusion

Sales tax is the most buoyant source of revenue for the States. The administration of sales tax varies across the States in terms of fixing rate of tax, exemptions, point of levy, multiplicity of tax rates, tax laws and assessment procedures. Central sales tax is another levy on inter-State sale of goods. Even though the basic intentions of the CST Act are good but the burden of bearing this rate as well as the usual tax rates of the importing States is unduly heavy. Hence, there is a need for tax harmonization of sales tax rates in India so as to ensure uniformity. Value added tax is a multipoint levy on the value added at each stage of the production and consumption of goods and services.

Endnotes

1. Purohit, Mahesh (1975), "Sales Taxation in India: An Economic Analysis of its Structure and Operations with Special Reference to the Northern Zone", S. Chand & Co., New Delhi, pp. 12-18.
2. Sree, Kantaradhya (2000), "Structure and Reforms of Taxation in India", Deep and Deep Publications Pvt. Ltd., New Delhi, p. 128.
3. Purohit, Mahesh (1982), "Structure of Sales Tax in India", *Economic and Political Weekly*, Mumbai, August 21, 1982, pp. 1365-1375.
4. Government of India (1953-54), "Taxation Enquiry Commission (TEC), 1953-54", Ministry of Finance, Vol. III, para 17.
5. Rao, Govinda M. (2003), "Reform of Central Sales Tax in the Context of VAT", *Economic and Political Weekly*, Mumbai, February 15, 2003, pp. 627-636.
6. Chelliah, Raja et al. (2001), "Primer on Value Added Tax", National Institute of Public Finance and Policy, New Delhi, p. 59.
7. Government of India (1978), "Report of the Indirect Taxation Enquiry Committee", Part I, October 1977, Ministry of Finance, p. 54.
8. Government of India (1991), "Tax Reforms Committee", Interim Report, Ministry of Finance, New Delhi, p. 124.
9. NIPFP (1984), "Reform of Domestic Trade Taxes in India: Issues and Options", New Delhi, India, p. 1.
10. Rao, Govinda M. (2003), "Reform of Central Sales Tax in the Context of VAT", *Economic and Political Weekly*, Mumbai, February 15, 2003, pp. 627-636.

11. Government of India (1978), "Report of the Indirect Taxation Enquiry Committee", Ministry of Finance, Part II, p. 20.
12. NIPFP (1984), "Reform of Domestic Trade Taxes in India: Issues and Options", New Delhi, India, p. 29.
13. NIPFP (1994), "Reform of Domestic Trade Taxes in India: Issues and Options", New Delhi, India, p. 33.
14. NIPFP (1995), "Report of the Committee of State Finance Ministers on Sales Tax Reform", New Delhi, p. 8.
15. NIPFP (1995), "The Report of the Committee of State Finance Ministers on Sales Tax Reform", New Delhi, p. 9.
16. Government of India (1978), "Report of the Indirect Taxation Enquiry Committee", Ministry of Finance, Part II, p. 222.
17. Purohit, Mahesh (1975), "Sales Tax Exemptions in India", *Economic and Political Weekly*, Mumbai, March 8, pp. 445-452.
18. NIPFP (1995), "Report of the Committee of State Finance Ministers on Sales Tax Reform", New Delhi, p. 15.

5

Value Added Tax (VAT)

The national income (gross domestic product) of a country for a fiscal year is estimated as the gross output of goods and services produced within the territorial boundaries of the country. Since goods pass through various stages until they reach the final consumer, the total value of a good is measured as the totality of the values created at each stage of production.

Carl S. Shoup defines VAT as a tax on the value added by a business firm, through its own activity for the goods and services it buys from other business firms.

Value added tax is a levy on the value added at each stage of production and distribution and essentially becomes a multipoint tax. In simple words, it is a tax on the difference between the sale value and the purchase value. If a company purchases raw materials and equipment for ₹ 500 and sells the output and services for ₹ 800, then the value added is ₹ 800-₹ 500 = ₹ 300. Since the burden of tax is borne by the final consumer and is not a charge on companies, it is a consumption tax.

As VAT is levied as a percentage of sale value (price), the actual tax burden is visible at each stage of production and distribution. In other words, VAT is a multistage tax where the tax is levied on the value added at each stage and not on the gross value of the dealer. It is taxation of inputs once only since it passes through various stages until it reaches the final consumer and is not cumulative as is in the case of turnover tax.

5.1 Introduction of VAT

Being a federal country, India has the advantage of a huge common market. Economies to scale and cost efficient production of goods and services can be achieved in such large common markets if there are no barriers to trade and there is free flow of factors of production within the federation. Since prices of goods and services are uniform across the states under the common market, the demand for goods is the aggregate demand of all state economies and the production becomes integrated, which in turn triggers the level of goods to be produced. Consumers will benefit from the increased competition from sellers and from realization of economies to scale through the concentration of productive activities.

On the other hand, some producers in some states, with competitive advantage in terms of infrastructure, largely benefit from the common market while others suffer in the short-term with uncompetitive industries, which would undergo restructuring and gain in the long-term. Hence, in large federal countries, free mobility of labour and capital across the states tend to homogenize the variant marginal productivities in different states, leading to efficient allocation of resources.

Inter-state jurisdictional competition in providing infrastructure and tax benefits across the states will attract capital that will lead to the adoption of improved technologies. Hence, federal countries have the advantage of not only ensuring efficient utilization of resources but also in adopting new innovations resulting in increased economic growth and the resultant prosperity for the citizens.

Some States have erected trade barriers to protect the local trade and industry by restricting exports and imports from the state through fiscal policies. With regard to migration of labour, some of the State governments even imposed the knowledge of local language as a pre-condition for employment in government sector enterprises in their States. Some North-Eastern States prohibit outsiders to engage in trade and commerce unless they have a local partner. Restrictions on the inter-State sale of oilseeds in Gujarat and raw cashewnuts in Kerala and monopoly procurement of cotton in Maharastra are some of the trade restrictions which act as barriers to free trade. Some States offered concessions to industries only if they employ the locals. Karnataka fixed 80 percent employment opportunities for the local persons. Such non-fiscal barriers are of lesser evil as compared to fiscal barriers such as inter-State and intra-State taxation.

Goods entering local areas for consumption or sale are usually taxed, such as the imposition of octroi in some States, viz. Gujarat, Haryana, Maharashtra, Odisha and West Bengal. Karnataka and Madhya Pradesh have replaced octroi by entry tax. The efficiency has been lost due to imposition of octroi or entry tax since they act as impediments to the free flow of traffic and are instrumental in rampant corruption, harassment of tax payers, perfuctionery assessment of the tax based on trust rather than actual books of account and multiple taxation of same goods in different urban local bodies.

The Central Government, on its part, instead of preventing unhealthy competition between the States rather promoted the "race to bottom" policies indulged by some Union Territories such as Puducherry, Chandigarh and Daman and Diu whose policies are decided by the Union Home Ministry. The lower tax rates for motor vehicles set by these union territories distorted the sales tax system in the neighbouring States and these States erected additional barriers in the name of entry tax for vehicles registered outside the State. The enactment of 46th Amendment to the Constitution empowering States to tax consignment transfers is another instance where the Centre facilitated the exportation of tax in spite of the fact that inter-State taxation was initially imposed on a maximum rate of 1 percent to prevent the evasion of local sales tax by claiming it as an inter-State sale.

Fortunately, the Constitution of India recognised the importance of common market, as enunciated under Article 301, which states, "Subject to other provisions of this part, trade, commerce and intercourse throughout the country shall be free". In meeting the exigencies, Article 302 empowers the Parliament to impose such restrictions on the freedom to trade, commerce and intercourse between one State and another or within any part of the territory of India as may be required in public interest.

5.2 Central VAT

This is similar to the VAT implemented in some countries such as Argentina, Germany, Austria and Mexico where the federal government administers the VAT covering all goods and services and the collection of revenue is entrusted either to the states or to the centre or both with a predetermined revenue sharing formula. Since the central government administers the VAT, the rate of tax is uniform throughout the country and the taxpayers would be left with a single set of VAT rules that improves tax compliance and efficiency in administration. But, in India, revenue sharing creates problems, as State sales tax revenues constitute more than 60 percent of their own tax revenue. Hence, it is highly unlikely that the States could agree to vacate their most buoyant source of revenue following their bitter experiences with the Centre on the previous rental arrangement of imposing additional excise in lieu of sales tax on tobacco, sugar and textile which still remains. Also, it will increase the dependency of States on the Centre for additional resources.

5.2.1 Dual VAT: As the Centrally administered VAT would not be acceptable politically for the States, it would increase the fiscal dependence of the States. A feasible solution in the short-term is to have a dual VAT in which both the Centre and the States concurrently administer VAT. The Tax Reforms Committee (1991) [1] headed by R.J. Chelliah recommended a dual VAT in which the CENVAT on excises at the Central level would be extended to the wholesale level under the condition that the States should administer VAT at the wholesale stage and retain the proceeds. In spite of its advantages, this proposal requires the Constitutional amendment as well as coordination between States in identifying the bonafide dealers dispatching and receiving goods. In the current scenario, it is possible to have an independent dual VAT where the Central government continues to have existing union excise duty as Central VAT up to the manufacturing level and the existing sales tax in States as State VAT.

The NIPFP (1993) study team also recommended a dual VAT comprising of the Central and the State VAT within the ambit of Constitutional framework. The team recommended that the Central excise will be converted into a manufacturing VAT by expanding the base in all goods manufactured, imported and a few select services. It also recommended that full input tax credit be given along with the simplified tax structure with less than three rates. States on the other hand have widened the tax base by reducing exemptions and including services, converting the tax into a multistage levy with credit given for tax on purchases and for tax on all inputs and capital goods. The TRC defined wholesaler as a dealer engaged in the production of excisable goods with an annual turnover of more than ₹ 50 lakh or ₹ 1 crore.

5.2.2 State VAT: Under State VAT system, the Centre has to vacate from the domestic trade taxation while retaining a small number of high revenue yielding excise goods. The States are entrusted to administer their own VAT to replace their current sales tax system in addition to the union excise on many goods. Burgess, Howes and Stern (1993), [2] suggested that it is possible to design versions of this proposal that are broadly revenue neutral between the Centre and the States. Also, it is politically attractive for the States as well as to reduce dependency on the Centre and in the long run it would promote fiscal responsibility and discipline on the part of the States. But in the short run, it would impair the Centre's ability to undertake redistribution and would result in the five poorest States loosing up to 40 percent of their budgets and the nine richest major States gaining by the same extent.

Joshi and Little (1996), [3] suggested a proposal in which the States may be entrusted with a broad-based VAT at a single rate leaving a handful of demerit and luxury goods such as alcohol, tobacco, petrol, diesel fuels and motor cars to the Central excises. They worked out the gains and losses for the Centre and the States and found that the Centre's grant to States of 2.19 percent of the GDP is marginally higher than the present 2.12 percent. According to the proposal, the State's VAT would preserve the fiscal autonomy of the States, permit inter-State redistribution and maintain desirable qualities of VAT and efficient administration. Later, Rao and Nirvikar Singh (1988), [4] worked out the redistributive implications of Joshi-Little proposal and estimated the revenue loss to the tune of ₹ 3,500 crore for the States whose SDP is less than the average per capita SDP. The better off States tended to gain ₹ 1,700 crore. Further, they stated that the richer States would benefit more if services were brought under taxation due to administrative efficiency.

5.3 Progress of Reforming State Sales Tax system

In order to reform the State sales tax structure, the Union Finance Ministry set up an Empowered Committee of ten State Finance Ministers headed by the West Bengal Finance Minister Mr. Asim Das Gupta to find ways and means to achieve a coordinated sales tax structure in India. The Finance Ministers Committee submitted its report in 1995 listing out sequence of steps to convert the present State sales tax system into a consumption type destination VAT.

As a first step, the Committee fixed four floor rates of 0, 4, 8 and 12 percent for general commodities and additionally two tax rates of 1 and 20 percent for a few specific items. These floor rates were the minimum tax rates and the States were given the freedom to set higher than these floor rates, but not below it. These floor rates were fixed to curb the inter-State rate wars and to prevent diversion of trade. Some States encountered problems in implementing these floor rates due to classification ambiguities and administrative difficulties. In this respect, the report of the Finance Ministers Committee [5] (1995), stated, "fine tuning of these classifications would have to be done by a special group". The Empowered Committee brought out three rates of 0 percent, 4 percent and a revenue neutral rate of (RNR) of 12.5 percent for implementation of VAT in all States.

Secondly, the Committee recommended the abolition of sales tax incentives being offered by States to attract new industries and trade in the form of waivers and deferrals which should be discontinued for all the new industries likely to be set up in the future in order to prevent the unhealthy tax competition or harmful tax practices, as these 'race to bottom' policies reduces nearly 25 percent of tax bases of the States.

During the third and final stage, efforts should be taken up to relieve the taxation of inputs and capital goods in addition to further rate rationalization and ultimate abolition of inter-State sales tax. Following these recommendations, many State governments initiated several steps to rationalise their tax structure such as Andhra Pradesh, Kerala, Rajasthan and West Bengal and extended their taxation beyond first point while other States seriously deliberated on this issue. From January 1, 2000, many States adjusted a uniform 4 floor rate structure (0, 4, 8 and 12 percent) and stopped all incentives to new industrial units.

After Herculean efforts over a decade and postponements, 20 of the States in India have switched over to a system of value added tax replacing their existing sales tax system with only a handful of States such as Gujarat, Madhya Pradesh, Tamil Nadu, Uttar Pradesh and Rajasthan staying out due to extraneous reasons. At the State level, replacing the sales tax system with VAT is regarded as the boldest tax reform undertaken in independent India. The half a century old sales taxes levied by the States was quite complex and VAT has mitigated these complex structure in taxation. The first point sales taxation with its multiple forms such as surcharges, turnover tax and additional sales tax, etc. has distorted the indirect taxation in India and the multiplicity of tax rates often lead to confusion in drawing distinctions among goods that were often flawed and led to endless disputes.

During the Budget Speech for the year 2005-06, the Union Finance Minister Mr. P. Chidambaram, announced that his government would implement value added tax from April 01, 2005. On January 17, 2005, a White Paper [6] released by the Empowered Committee outlined the basic structure of State VAT. Some of the important features of a uniform State VAT as brought out by the White Paper are given below.

1. There will be uniform tax rates on approximately 550 commodities generally traded in India.
2. There will be uniform tax rates of 4 percent and 12.5 percent in addition to a 1 percent rate in case of precious stones and precious metals with an exemption of 46 items.
3. The maximum threshold limit was fixed at ₹ 5 lakh. These dealers whose turnover falls below the threshold limit, are exempted from VAT. All remaining exemption would be withdrawn.
4. VAT credits were allowed for all tax paid on purchases within the States from the VAT payable by a dealer and covered all raw materials, capital foods and items purchased for resale by the registered dealers. For those dealers whose total turnover lies between ₹ 5 lakh and ₹ 50 lakh, they can opt for a simple composition scheme in which such dealers would be allowed to pay a nominal tax on their total turnover without taking any credit for tax paid on purchases under the VAT system.
5. Exports and sale to special economic zones would be zero-rated.
6. VAT credit would be available on purchase of input materials and capital goods.
7. No credit would be allowed for taxes paid on purchases made outside a particular State.
8. States can continue with the existing sales tax incentives committed earlier without breaking the VAT chain.
9. The opening stocks as on April 1, 2005 would be eligible for input tax credit provided such purchases are made

within a period of one year prior to this date, i.e. after March 31, 2004.

The feature of VAT uniformity agreed by the States is a major step in the direction of reforming State taxes and is considered as a major step towards harmonization of State sales tax system (Table 5.1).

Table 5.1: Implementation of VAT by Indian States

State	Date of Implementation
Haryana	April 1, 2003
Arunachal Pradesh, Assam , Himachal Pradesh, Mizoram, Nagaland ,New Delhi, Sikkim, Tripura Goa, Jammu and Kashmir, Manipur Andhra Pradesh, Bihar, Haryana, Karnataka, Kerala, Maharashtra, Odisha, Punjab, West Bengal, Meghalaya	April 1, 2005
Uttarkhand	October 1, 2005
Rajasthan, Jharkhand, Chhatisgarh, Madhya Pradesh, Gujarat	April 1, 2006
Tamil Nadu	January 1, 2007
Uttar Pradesh	January 1, 2008

The success of VAT in Indian states is the cumulative effect of growing state economies, strict enforcement and improvements in the voluntary compliance. Now the state sales tax collection authorities have familiarised themselves with the tax concepts and the nuances of tax collection. Therefore, it is the right time to switchover to goods and service tax (GST) which is overdue, as the gains achieved in the implementation of state VAT may be exploited.

The successful implementation of VAT in 2005 by the States is hailed as the boldest innovative tax reform undertaken in the independent India. The design of VAT implemented was based on a study "Reform of Domestic Trade Taxes in India: Issues and Options" done by Amaresh Bagchi. Considering the fragile nature of the Centre-State financial relations, the study recommended a dual VAT: a Central VAT replacing the existing Central excise duty and a State VAT replacing the existing sales tax system in the States. The Report also clearly spelt out that dual VAT recommendation is only a short-term and feasible solution to the complex taxation system in India and the immediate implementation may pave the way for a more progressive, rational, destination-based consumption type taxation system covering both goods and services in the future.

5.3.1 Merits and Demerits of VAT: VAT is the appropriate mechanism to capture all these value additions. It is now up to the State sales tax machineries of various States to improve their collection efficiency. Joshua Aizeman and Yothin Jinjark (2005), [7] evaluated the political and structural factors on VAT collection efficiency and found that the political factors such as great polarization and political instability reduce tax collection efficiency whereas structural factors such as urbanization, share of agriculture and trade openness, improve tax collection efficiency.

In order to avoid the new problems and reap the benefits of taxation, VAT becomes imperative. The design of VAT that has been adopted by the States in India satisfies most of the properties of a good VAT with some shortcomings. Under the Indian Constitution, sales tax is a State subject and hence each State has its own law for VAT. However, in formulating VAT laws, States are required to follow the pattern laid down by the Committee of State Finance Ministers called the "Empowered Committee" (EC) entrusted with the task of facilitating the implementation of VAT in the States. The EC came out with a White Paper that laid down the scheme of VAT that the States had agreed to adopt as the basis for their respective legislations that is supposed to replace their sales tax laws.

The new VAT is a multi-stage taxation of sales with credit for VAT paid on inputs, and, in most cases, full credit will be allowed. Only the tax paid on capital goods may be spread out over two or three years. As such, the credit should be available to all registered dealers instantaneously in such a way that the dealers can take credit in their accounts and pay only the net amount due after setting off the taxes paid on their purchases or inputs. VAT laws of some States have set up a time frame for refunds to be paid ranging from six months to two years. In spite of these merits, there are other problems which are enumerated below.

A serious demerit is the exclusion of services. Under the Seventh Schedule of the Constitution, the power of sales taxation is restricted only to goods. The Centre, using the residual Entry in the Union list, is taxing selected services since 1994.

After the Constitutional Amendment carried out in 2003, the Centre has acquired power to tax services. But it is still unclear whether the Centre would allocate selected services to the States and its eventual integration with the VAT. Hence, due to the non-inclusion of services, State VAT suffers from a major drawback of narrow base and violates neutrality.

5.4 Suggestions

The disentanglement of tax rates envisaged in the White Paper could have been avoided if the general rate was fixed at a lower level, say 8 to 10 percent, regarded as the 'floor rate' and the States may choose a higher rate if they so wish and a reduced rate of 4 percent or 5 percent was prescribed for only a few commodities of local or basic consumption with the exception of inputs.

Also, the reduced rate should have been specified as a floor rate and not mandated to be uniform across the States. This would mean that there can be variation of rates across States subject to a floor rate but there would be basically only one rate in each State by allowing the States to choose a higher rate if they so desired. For the sake of simplicity, businesses and industry want a single or at most two rates to be applied to all commodities uniformly across all the States.

However, it should be realised that India's polity is federal in structure with powers and functions divided between two levels of government. For efficient functioning of such a system, it is necessary that the constituent units should not only have responsibilities for providing services that are best delivered at sub-national levels, but they should also have access to revenue sources of their own. In order that the sub-national governments behave responsibly in the matter of spending, they must be able to control the level of revenue they require at the margin, and for that they must be able to set the level of taxes to correspond with the prospects of their voters. As is known, sub-national taxation can give rise to 'externalities' such as the thorough tax competition that occurred in India under the sales tax regime and is happening now with States failing to adhere to the floor rate for many commodities. Hence, some coordination or harmonization becomes imperative when tax powers are vested with the States.

However, tax harmonization, which may require uniformity in base and procedures, should not extend to the choice of tax rates. [8] It should be noted that uniformity of rates across the States is not a requirement for establishment of a common market. The common market needs tax-free movement of goods and services across States that are best served through a destination-based VAT provided all States adhere to a floor rate. The 'floor rate' serves to check the devastating tax competition among the States while no State can go in for unduly high rates, or otherwise business will move away from its territory.

As for as the European Union is concerned, even though the businesses and industry want a single rate to be applied to all commodities uniformly across all states where the destination-based VAT constitutes a major plank for the common market, its Sixth Directive mandates uniformity. But, it should be realized that India's polity is federal in structure with powers and functions separated between two levels of government with their respective fiscal autonomy. European

Union continues to thrive on a common market with only a floor rate for the standard commodities and reduced rates for the rest.

Functioning of a common market requires that there is no taxation of inter-state trade. The destination principle seems to serve this objective by requiring that either no tax is levied on inter-state sales by the states of origin, or the tax so levied is rebated in the state of destination for final consumption. The White Paper of the EC suggests that the system of State VAT will be based on the destination principle as the CST will be phased out in the next two years. But operating such a VAT in a federal country like India is not simple as zero rating opens up opportunities for fraud—as dealers may find it lucrative to disguise sales within a State as inter-State.

To guard against such misuse, the system that has evolved in India so long is that a registered dealer claiming to have sold any good to a registered dealer outside the State has to produce evidence in support of the claim. A special form known as "C-form" is prescribed for this purpose and has to be obtained by a vendor selling goods inter-State from the purchasing dealer. The C-form enables him to charge tax at the CST rate on the sale. When the CST gets abolished and inter-State sales are zero-rated, the opportunity for fraud will be accentuated and so a system has to be devised which can counter this tendency. In fact, because of this difficulty in operating a destination-based VAT in a federation, it was often suggested that VAT is best administered at the national level as has been done in Australia.

The EU had to grapple with this problem when in 1993 'fiscal frontiers' within the Union were abolished. Until then, zero-rating on inter-country sales within the Union was practiced on the strength of customs documents supporting movement of goods from one member country to another. The way zero-rating operates now in EU is the following: when goods are sold by a (registered) dealer in say France to one in Germany, the dealer in France zero rates the sale as it is.

Under the system prevalent at present for inter-State sales taxation, there is an incentive for abuse in that the maximum rate of CST applicable to B2B sales is 4 percent, whereas the rate of tax on many commodities sold within a State goes well beyond 4 percent in all States for purchases originating in the EU and allowing member countries to tax B2C sales at rates of their choice (subject to a floor rate). The revenue from B2B sale would be pooled and shared by member countries, based on their consumption data (Keen and Smith, 2000). [9] This suggestion though favoured by some experts, has not been acted upon so far.

In Canada, a federal level VAT called the goods and services tax (GST) has been in operation since 1991 along with retail sales taxes in several provinces and a provincial VAT in one viz. Quebec. Three maritime provinces have gone in for a system of harmonized VAT whereby the federal government levies GST at the prescribed rate (7 percent) and along with it, a provincial VAT (8 percent). Recently, a Task Force set up by the Ministry of Finance in India under Mr. Vijay Kelkar which has suggested the imposition of a GST by the Central government to run in parallel with VAT to be levied by the States on the same base. [10]

However, for reasons stated earlier, if the States are to retain their fiscal autonomy in this vital area of taxation, they should have the power to fix the rates applicable to sales within their territory. As the excise duties levied by the government in the form of Central VAT (CENVAT) applies only at the manufacturing stage, the system proposed by the Kelkar Task Force would require amending the Constitution to enable the Centre to tax sales up to the retail stage.

While this seems to be a promising alternative and has been widely welcomed, the precise form in which it will operate e.g., whether the State VAT will run in parallel with GST, and whether the two will be administered by one authority viz., the Centre or by both Centre and the States, will need to be worked out in greater detail and their pros and cons debated in greater depth. For now, the endeavour is to see that the glaring flaws in the design of the State VAT that have just come into operation, are removed and that they run well. That will call for creating an authority that can enforce the decisions arrived at by the States through the EC or its successor.

In the EU, the Sixth Directive is binding on all member countries and others can contest any deviation in the European Court of Justice. The White Paper drawn up by the EC holds out a threat to errant States that deviations will be reported to the Centre who, presumably will then use its clout ('transfer' power) to punish the 'guilty'—in other words, by arm twisting to get them 'behave'. This is scarcely healthy for a federal system. Our Constitution contains a clear mandate that trade, commerce and intercourse throughout the Union shall be free (Article 301)—obviously a mandate for a common market for India.

5.5 Conclusion

VAT achieves efficiency, cascading, easy enforcement, transparency and is simple. The feature of VAT uniformity agreed by the States is a major step in the direction of reforming State taxes and is considered as a major step towards harmonization of State sales tax system. The introduction of VAT at the State level replacing the complex sales taxes is hailed as the boldest tax reform measure implemented in the Independent India. Even though most of the States implemented VAT since April 2005, VAT still suffers from shortcomings such as exclusion of services from VAT base, no input credits for Inter-State trade, etc. The major problem will arise when zero-rating of CST comes into effect to achieve a common market for India. In such a case, the European model provides a solution that the revenue from inter-State sales may be pooled and shared by the States based on their consumption data.

Endnotes

1. Government of India (1991), "Tax Reforms Committee", Ministry of Finance, Part II, p. 45.

2. Burgess, R. and N. Stern (1993), "Tax Reforms in India", Working Paper No. 45, STICERD, London School of Economics.
3. Joshi, V. and I.M.D. Little (1996), "India's Economic Reforms: 1991-2001", Oxford University Press, New Delhi.
4. Rao, Govinda and Nirvikar Singh (1998), "Fiscal Overlapping, Concurrency and Competition in Fiscal Federalism", Centre for Research on Economic Development and Policy, Stanford University.
5. NIPFP (1995), "Report of the State Finance Ministers Committee on Rationalisation of Sales Tax".
6. Government of India (2005), "A White Paper on State Level Value Added Tax", Ministry of Finance, New Delhi, January 17, 2005.
7. Joshua, Aizeman and Yothin Jinjarak (2005), "The Collection Efficiency of the Value Added Tax: Theory and International Evidence", Working Paper No. 11539, National Bureau of Economic Research, Cambridge.
8. McLure, C.E. (2000), "Implementing Sub-national Value Added Tax on Internal Trade: The Compensating VAT (CVAT)", *International Tax and Public Finances*, 7(6), pp. 723-740.
9. Keen, Michael and P. Smith (2000), "Viva VIVAT!", *International Tax and Public Finance*, Elsevier, Toronto, Vol. 6, pp. 741-751.
10. Kelkar, Vijay (2003), Task Force on Indirect Taxes, Ministry of Finance, Government of India.

6

Services Tax

6.1 Introduction

Service sector is one of the rapidly growing areas of economic activity comprising all kinds of activities such as banking, insurance, hospitality, wholesale, distribution, retailing, research and development, etc. This sector holds a predominant position among the economies world over. Due to the globalization of economies during the past two decades, its percentage contribution to gross domestic product (GDP) has increased to more than 50 percent in most of the developing and developed countries of the world. By taking advantage of the faster increase in world trade and absorption of huge foreign direct investment (FDI), service sector has grown by leaps and bounds and holds nearly 25 percent of the world merchandise exports. [1]

Now, it becomes synonymous to state that the growth of services is closely associated with the growth of the economy. Major changes in the structure of services to GDP happened from 1995-96 to 2004-05. Trade continued to lead as the largest contributor to services GDP by accounting for 27.5 percent of services GDP. In 2004-05, public administration, dwellings, road transport, education, banks and business services were the major contributors to services GDP. Other important services accounting for over two percent of the services GDP were hotel and restaurants, non-banking financial institutions and public sector communications (2.1 percent).The services sector is a highly non-homogeneous sector comprising a wide range of activities. There are differences within the services sector with regard to the contribution of different sub-sectors to GDP and to the employment. In the contemporary world, services have become a major contributor to the GDP in most developed as well as developing countries. The multifarious activities of the services sector have some special feature of non-storability, non-tradability and intangibility.

6.2 Growth of GDP and Share of Services Sector

In India, the growth of service sector during the post-reforms period posted an average growth rate of 8.2 percent which is primarily responsible for the faster increase in the overall economy as is evident from Table 6.1.

It is apparent from the Table that the percentage contribution from the service sector to the GDP is steadily growing in India from a mere 38 percent in 1971-72 to 57 percent in 2015-16. During the same period, the growth of services surpassed the traditional sectors of agriculture and industry.

Table 6.1: Percentage Share and Annual Growth Rate of Various Sectors of the Economy

	Percentage Contribution to GDP			Annual Growth Rate (percent)			
Year	A	I	S	A	I	S	GDP
1971-72	46	16	38	-1.9	3.6	3.1	0.9
1981-82	40	18	43	5.3	8.8	5.4	6.0
1991-92	31	21	48	-1.5	-1.2	4.5	1.3
2000-01	24	22	54	-0.1	6.5	5.6	4.4
2001-02	24	22	54	6.5	3.5	6.4	5.8
2004-05	19	28	53	0.2	9.8	8.3	7.1
2005-06	18	28	54	5.1	9.7	10.9	9.5
2006-07	17	29	54	4.2	12.2	10.1	9.6
2007-08	17	29	54	5.8	9.7	10.3	9.3
2008-09	16	28	56	0.1	4.1	10.0	6.7
2009-10	15	28	57	0.8	9.2	10.5	8.6
2010-11	15	28	57	8.6	7.6	9.7	8.9
2011-12	14	28	57	5.0	7.8	6.6	6.7
2012-13	14	27	59	1.2	2.3	8.0	5.1
2013-14	14	26	60	3.7	4.5	9.1	6.9
2014-15	14	26	60	1.1	5.9	10.6	7.6
2015-16	14	29	57	1.1	7.3	9.2	7.6

A = Agriculture; I = Industry; S = Services

Source: National Accounts Statistics (various years).

6.3 Rationale

Whenever the tax base is narrow, there is every possibility of taxing close substitutes or persons with equal stature, being taxed differently. This horizontal inequality will in turn enhance the possibility of causing economic distortions. Also, higher tax rates have to be imposed with a narrow base than a broader tax base. Hence, a broader tax base by including services in the general sales tax base is imperative for fairness and economic efficiency. The most important reason for taxing services is the potential and stable source of revenue inherent in the system as the consumption of services is more stable than the consumption of consumer goods with the changing economic circumstances. Generally, governments favour steady flow of revenues, as government activities require committed flow of funds for many years. Instability in government revenues often makes it impossible for long-term planning. Hence, from the stability point of view, taxation of services became imperative. In terms of efficiency, taxation of services reduces the potential distortion of sales tax at the point of sale when the consumer is deciding between goods and services.

When a tax free service is available as a substitute for a taxable consumer good, consumers are left with a choice in selecting a service or a good accordingly to the consumer's resource allocation—as when the repairing services are not taxed, the consumers might go for repairing consumer durables instead of purchasing a new one. Hence, exclusion of services distorts allocation of scarce resources. Therefore, from the efficiency point of view, services should be brought under sales taxation. On the equity consideration, there is a strong and valid basis for taxing services, as most of the services are luxuries, and hence taxing services becomes taxing luxuries. It can be proved empirically regards the existence of a direct relationship between the personal incomes and the expenditure on consumption of services. From Table 6.2, the consumption of services increases as the income level increases both in rural and urban areas. With this direct relationship, taxation of services becomes imperative.

Table 6.2: Consumption Expenditure on Services (2002)

Expenditure Group (per capita per month) (₹)	Rural (₹)	Urban (₹)
0-300	6.60	11.53
300-350	8.56	13.19
350-425	10.12	16.82
425-500	12.86	21.39
500-575	15.20	27.03
575-665	17.89	34.90
665-775	20.94	47.95
775-915	24.92	71.74
915-1,120	31.36	92.43
1,120-1,500	46.89	148.06
1,500-1,925	66.87	225.61
1,925 and more	138.88	531.41

Source: National Sample Survey Organisation, Tables of Consumer Expenditure, 58th Round (July 2002-December 2002), Department of Statistics, Government of India, New Delhi.

A study done by the National Institute of Public Finance and Policy in 1994 pointed out that services often become an integral part of manufacturing and trade and the line between goods and services is getting increasingly blurred such as development of software, desktop publishing, printing of photographs, etc. involves a variety of services such as training, installation and maintenance. By taking advantage of these definitional ambiguities, the manufacturers in collusion with traders underestimate the value of manufactured goods by claiming discounts for post-manufacturing services such as transportation, installation and maintenance. [2]

In case of sales taxes too, the first point taxation on goods where the base is free of services and trade margins tend to distort consumers and producers such items which carry higher trade margins are more favoured than the essential goods and the producers add more number of services to underestimate the value of their products. India, being a developing economy, is in need of huge funds to finance its development plans as well as to fulfil its ever increasing obligations to the people. It draws more than 60 percent revenue from its indirect taxes and less than 40 percent from direct taxes. Central excise duty and customs duty are the two main indirect taxes for the Central government. During the post-reforms period, a series of tax reform measures have been initiated to make the goods manufactured in India competitive in the global market by mitigating the cascading and complex tax system of consumption taxes. One such measure has been the implementation of CENVAT in central excise in which the instant credits are available on inputs used in the manufacturing.

As a result, revenue loss to the tune of 1.4 percent in terms of GDP costs the exchequer. Similarly, the government has gradually reduced the import duty on many categories of imports primarily on the commitments made to the World Trade Organization (WTO). Due to these reasons, revenue from these two indirect taxes suffered a steady decline during the post-reforms period. To compensate the loss due to the indirect taxes and to improve the tax-GDP ratio, taxes on services became imperative. Even though the agricultural sector contributes nearly 25 percent to the GDP, it is out of tax net.

Since services contribute more than one half to the GDP, it has to be taxed, as the manufacturing sector alone cannot be overburdened. Over burdening the manufacturing sector will have a negative impact on the competitiveness of this sector. Hence, it becomes imperative to tax services and its integration with goods. Also taxing goods alone breaches the neutrality in taxation and distorts consumer choice between good and services. Fiscal economists on the other hand argue that there is no good reason for not taxing services when goods are subjected to tax, as otherwise both efficiency and equity suffer. Efficiency, because by favouring services over goods, it tends to distort resource allocation and equity, because it benefits the rich more as they consume more of the services than the poor. [3]

The state governments, though they are not empowered to levy taxes on services, stretching beyond their powers, have imposed multiple levies such as luxury tax on hotels and restaurants, betting tax, lottery tax, entertainment tax, electricity duty, taxes on passengers and goods, etc. When VAT is introduced by merging services and goods, these multiple levies become a part and parcel of the VAT and the tax system will become simple. Hence, not only from the point of view of improving the revenue productivity, but also from evolving an efficient, systematic and orderly taxation system without distortions, taxing services along with the goods became necessary and in most countries world over where value added tax was introduced, taxation was extended to both goods and services.

6.4 Services Tax in India

The Tax Reforms Committee (1991) [4] under the chairmanship of Dr. Raja Chelliah recommended that indirect taxes at the Central level should be broadly neutral in relation to production and consumption of goods, and should in course of time cover commodities and services. If further recommended that when Central excise duty on manufactured goods becomes a value added tax at the manufacturing level, service tax should also form an integral part of it. The Committee paid more attention towards a revenue neutral value added tax system that would reduce the cascading effect on consumers. The Committee further contended charging of tax in services to begin with on the pattern of advanced economies and the fundamental basis of service tax should be to widen the tax base and enhancing revenue and larger participation of citizens in the economic development of the nation.

As per the recommendations of the Tax Reforms Committee, the then the Union Finance Minister Dr. Manmohan Singh introduced service tax in India during 1994-95 and in his budget speech stated that "there is no sound reason for exempting services from taxation, therefore, I propose to made a modest effort in this direction by imposing a tax on services of telephones, non-life insurance and stock brokers". [5] Since, services are intangibles and a large number of service providers are entrenched well across the country, it becomes so difficult to bring many services under the tax net.

6.5 Coverage of Services

Initially when service tax was introduced in 1994, only three services (telephones, non-life insurance and stock brokers) were taxed under the Finance Act, 1994. Subsequently, under Finance Acts of 1996,1997,1998, 2001,2002 and 2003 additional services were added and the total number of services had gone up to 58 and 4 services such as goods transport operators, outdoor caterers, *pandal* and *shamiyana* contractors, *mandap* keepers and mechanized slaughter houses were excluded from tax from 1997-98. Table 6.3 gives the coverage of services over the years.

Table 6.3: Coverage of Services for Tax

Year	Services Added
1994	Telephone, non-life insurance and stock brokers.
1995	Advertising agencies, courier services, radio pager services.
1996	Consulting engineers, customs house agents, travel agents, tour operators, rental call operators, manpower recruiting agency, and mandap keepers.
1997	Architects, interior decorators, management consultants, practicing chartered accountants, practicing company secretaries, practicing cost accountants, real estate agents/consultants, credit rating agencies, private security agencies, market research agencies and under writer agencies.
1998	Scientific and technical consultancy services, photography, convention, telegraph, telex, facsimile (fax), online
1999	Information and database access or retrieval, video-tape production, accountants, sound recording, broadcasting, insurance auxiliary activity, banking and other financial services.
2000	Auxiliary services to life insurance, cargo handling, storage and warehousing services, event management, cable operators, beauty parlours, health and fitness cultures, fashion designer, rail travel agents, dry cleaning services.

Contd...

2001	Business auxiliary services, commercial training or coaching services, commissioning or installation services, franchise services, access of internet service by the internet cable, maintenance and repair services, technical testing and analysis and technical inspection and certification services.
2002	Transport of goods by road (earlier goods transport operators service re-introduced), outdoor caterer's service (re-introduced), pandal or shamiana service (re-introduced), airport services, transport of goods by air services, business exhibition services, construction services in relation to commercial or industrial building construction services in relation to commercial or industrial building.
2003	Intellectual property services, opinion poll services, TV or radio programme services, survey and exploration of minerals services, travel agent's services other than rail and air travel agents, forward contract services, transport of goods through pipe line or other conduit services, site preparation and clearance services, dredging services, survey and mapmaking services, cleaning services, membership of clubs and associations, packaging services, mailing list compilation and mailing services, construction services in relation to residential complexes.
2004	Registrar to an issue, share transfer agent, automated teller machine (ATM) operations, maintenance or management services, recovery services, sale of space or time for advertisement, sponsorship services, transport of passengers by air, transport of goods in containers by rail, business support services, auctioneers' service, public relation services, ship management service, internet telephony service, transport of passengers by cruise ship, credit card, debit card, charge card or other payment card related service.
2005	Telecommunication services, services in relation to mining, renting of immovable property for commercial purposes, service provided in relation to execution of a works contract, development and supply of content, asset management including portfolio, management and all forms of fund, management provided by service, providers other than those providing banking and other financial services, design services.
2006	Information technology software service used for business or commerce, management of investment under unit, Linked Insurance Plan (ULIP) Scheme, services provided by stock exchange, services provided by commodity exchange, services provided by processing and clearing house, supply of tangible goods for use.
2007	Cosmetic and plastic surgery services, services provided in relation to transport of coastal goods, goods through inland water including national waterways, legal consultancy services.
2008	Promotion, marketing, organising or assisting in organising games of chance including lottery, bingo or lotto, health services provided by hospitals or nursing homes for which payments are made by employers and health insurance companies, maintenance of medical records of business entity, brand ambassador services, permitting commercial use or exploitation of any event, services provided by electricity exchanges, permitting use of copyright in cinematographic films and sound recording, special services provided by builder etc. to the prospective buyers in a residential complex such as providing preferential location or external or internal development of complexes for extra charges.

6.6 Prospects of Service Tax in Future

Before studying the potential opportunities for service tax in India in future, it becomes imperative to understand the various sectors under the services and their growth during the post and pre-reform periods. The most remarkable feature of India's growth during the last decade is its services sector. Jim Gordon and Poonam Gupta (2003), [6] analysed the factors behind the growth of service sector in India and opined that the growth in the acceleration of services in the 1990s was mostly due to the fast growth in communication services, fiscal services, business services (IT) and community services. Service sector grew at a faster pace surpassing the traditional agriculture and industrial sectors and posted consistent growth over the years as it is less prone to the business cycles. The consistent and rapid rise in service sector fits the general notion of growth in developing economies that during the initial take-off period, both the industry and services grew faster than agriculture and later, services outperformed rest of the economy with a stagnant or declining industrial sector.

From Table 6.4, it is evident that the growth of this sector is more consistent and increasing as the average growth rate increased from 4.6 percent in 1980-81 to 8.6 percent during 2013-2014, and its performance is conspicuous between 1981-82 and 2013-2014 as the services sector is less prone to public policies and receives huge investments compared to industry.

As services comprise a number of activities, it becomes necessary to know the vital services, which have grown predominantly during this period. It is apparent from the Table that since 1980s, services sector has grown consistently and has changed the composition of GDP. The percentage share of service sector has steadily grown from 37.1 percent in 1980-81 to 57 percent in 2015-2016. In terms of growth rate, it has grows at 8.6 percent during the post-reforms period as against 6.6 during the pre-reforms period. Even though the services sector has grown at a higher rate, its growth has not been uniform across the various sub-sectors..

Table 6.4: Share and Growth Rate of Various Services in India

S. No.	Description of Service	Share (percent)		
		1999-2000	2004-05	2009-10
1.	Trade	21.5	29.8	24.3
2.	Hotels and restaurants	1.8	3.0	2.3
3.	All transports	11.6	12.6	11.3
4.	Storage	0.1	0.1	0.1
5.	Communications	1.6	3.1	6.2
6.	Banking and insurance	11.6	10.8	13.7
7.	Real estate	0.6	0.4	0.4
8.	Business services	1.7	5.2	9.2
9.	Community services	11.6	11.3	10.9
10.	Public administration	14.5	14.1	12.4
11.	All other services	23.4	9.6	9.2
	Total services sector	100	100	100

Contd...

S. No.	Description of Service	Growth Rate (percent)		
		1979-80 to 1995-96	1995-96 to 2004-05	2004-05 to 2009-10
1.	Trade	6.4	10.7	9.1
2.	Hotels and restaurants	7.0	12.8	8.5
3.	All transports	6.3	7.6	8.0
4.	Storage	2.8	2.1	8.0
5.	Communications	8.1	20.7	26.7
6.	Banking and insurance	9.5	8.5	15.6
7.	Real estate	3.8	5.0	26.0
8.	Business services	10.7	21.3	17.2
9.	Community services	6.0	8.5	7.9
10.	Public administration	5.4	6.3	9.2
11.	All other services	6.6	6.3	1.1
	Total services sector	6.5	7.7	10.3

Source: Central Statistical Organisation.

In fact, at the sub-sector level, trade, hotels and restaurants, communication, business services, financial services and community services exhibited an increasing trend in their growth rates during the pre- and post-reforms period. But some sectors like business services became the fastest growing sector during the post-reforms period, with an average growth rate of nearly 20 percent. Among the sub-sectors, computer and related services with a share of 3.3 percent in India's GDP grew by 14.4 percent in 2013-14. The contribution of tourism to total income and employment of the country during 2012-13 was 6.9 percent and 12.5 percent respectively. In 2014, foreign tourist arrivals and foreign exchange earnings increased by 7.1 percent and 6.6 percent respectively. Communication grew at a rate of 14 percent with telecom being the major component. This sector has made significant contribution to the services sector.

Banking, communication, trade, hotels and restaurants, business services and community services witnessed acceleration in growth during the 1990s due to the economic reform measures, especially in the industrial sector where the rising manufacturing growth have driven higher demand for producer services. Ultimately, the fast growing services sector has come to occupy a dominant position with a share of 57 percent in the GDP in 2015-2016.

6.7 IT and IT-enabled Services

Technological advances in some sectors such as information technology (IT) and telecommunication has benefited India in exports of services. In India, exports of services in terms of US dollars grew at an average rate of 15 percent during the 1990s as against 9 percent during 1980s. Software development and information technology enabled services have emerged as one of the dynamic and vibrant sectors.

In the global outsourcing arena, India maintains its lead by cornering more than 50 percent of the global market. By 2013, service exports attained a figure of US$ 86 billion, being 35 percent of the total exports and one-third being contributed by software exports. The export of software and other related businesses continued to post rapid growth during 2000s.

The information technology sector grew at an annual rate of 20 percent between 1998 and 2013 and its turnover was estimated to be about US$ 105 billion in 2014.

The IT sector can be broadly categorized as software and

services (ITS) comprising systems integration, packaged software support and installation, application outsourcing, custom application development, etc. and IT-enabled services (ITES) like human resources, customer care, payment services, finance, etc. and hardware. During 1998-2013, the software exports market grew at an average rate of 42 percent and 16 percent for overseas and domestic markets respectively. As a result, the share of ITS and ITES exports in IT sector increased manifold and the relative share of domestic market for ITS and ITES fell down. The hardware segment's growth has however not been commensurate and its share has declined over this period. The composition and mode of delivery of IT exports has undergone change over this period. But over the years, the share of business process outsourcing (BPO) in IT exports has seen a substantial jump. In the mode of delivery of IT exports, there had been a perceptible change as more than half of all IT exports from India were carried out at onsite client spots and off shoring became the dominant mode of delivery of software exports as a percentage of total exports.

India has achieved the familiarity and experience with off shoring and this has dramatically increased the breadth of service lines. Significant under-penetrated segments exist at both country and industry levels and there is a pressure on global majors to outsource a significant portion of their work to India. The IT software and services industry is classified into four segments—IT services export sector, ITES exports, product and technology service and the domestic market. A broad spectrum of opportunities is available in areas like embedded software, development and delivery of specialized components, tapping offshore product development opportunities, product acquisition and enhanced and developed shrink-wrapped products. Another study by Deloitte Research pointed out that the global market in offshore financial services could grow to more than US$ 5,000 billion by 2015-16 of which a large share would go to India due to highly qualified professionals and educated people proficient in

English, lower labour costs, support extended by successive governments in terms of foreign direct investment, taxation and external trade.

In order to realise the full potential in IT sector, some of the barriers such as visa restrictions and negative publicity in importing countries affected by outsourcing may affect the future of IT exports from India. Moreover, the shortage of skilled manpower may pose a challenge as the sector expands—loss of cost advantage due to high demand for skilled IT professionals, appreciation of the Indian rupee, infrastructure constraints and internal issues within the industry are some of the problems that may grapple the Indian IT industry in future.

A recent survey conducted by the FICCI (Federation of Indian Chambers of Commerce and Industry) shows that retail industry holds massive potential and opportunities for growth and estimated the growth rate of this sector at 10 percent per annum.

The survey further stated that retail in India has grown beyond mere retailing as today it comprises of new sectors such as telecom, automobiles and finance. Services sector with a plethora of services having strong linkages to manufacturing, construction and transport and communication has provided the momentum for growth in housing and transport activities.

6.8 Tax Administration, Collection and Tasks Ahead

Central Excise Commissionerates under the control of Central Board of Excise and Customs, Department of Revenue, Ministry of Finance, Government of India is the authority for collection and administration of service tax. The most remarkable feature of service tax is the collection of tax through voluntary compliance. The Government adopted a lenient and flexible approach in order to gain faith and trust of the assessees to achieve voluntary compliance. Over the years, many measures have been taken to simplify the procedures. Even though initially, the rate of service tax was set at 5 percent on the value of taxable services, by 2003-3004, it had been raised to 8 percent. As per the Union Budget 2004-2005, it was increased to 10 percent and further increased to 14 percent from 2015-2016.

Service tax was levied on the gross amount charged by the service provider to the receiver. Later, it was modified as in some cases, the entire amount charged by the service providers may not have been received by the service provider and asking them to pay the tax on the charged amount in advance was against the very scheme of voluntary compliance. Initially, the frequency of paying tax and filing returns was fixed on a quarterly basis for the individuals whereas for corporate assesses, it was the 25th of every succeeding month.

However, later it was modified as half-yearly and by the 25th of the succeeding month following the half-year for both individual and corporate assesses and the Superintendent of the Central Excise was authorized to scrutinize the returns filed. The power to conduct field surveys to add more assesses is vested with the Central Excise Officers under the overall technical and policy guidance of the Directorate of Service Tax at Mumbai. Registration procedure has been simplified. No separate accounting procedure is prescribed and self-assessment procedure has been introduced for tax returns, so as to relieve the assessees from routine assessment and scrutiny. Penal provisions for failure to pay the tax and filing of returns has also been introduced.

However, no penalty is imposed on the assessee if a prima facie case exists for the course of the failure. In the case of prosecutions, Sections 87 to 93 of the Finance Act, 1994, introduced earlier have been withdrawn as a noble gesture towards the assesses. Finance Bill, 2002 empowers to allow input credits on services tax so as to avoid cascading impact of tax and to make the services sector competitive. This is a welcome step towards improving the tax compliance level and reducing disputes in tax administration.

As the services sector has grown at a decent rate, it provides ample opportunities to bring greater number of services under the tax net—the task ahead of administering the service tax is tremendous. The revenue potential of this sector will be huge and it will be a hunting ground for the government in the future. In the long-run, tax on services will reduce the unfair tax burden on the domestic trade taxes such as customs duty and central excise and would make the goods manufactured in India competitive in the global market. Hence, a coordinated and planned growth of service tax would be commensurate with the goals of economic liberalization and globalization. [7] Having recognized the revenue potential of the services sector, the government constituted a Task Force on Direct and Indirect Tax Reforms under the chairmanship of Mr. Vijay L. Kelkar. The Committee [8] recommended the following.

1. Service tax should be levied comprehensively leaving out a specific negative list of exempted and merit goods.
2. Integration of both CENVAT credit and service tax credits.
3. The rate of service tax should achieve parity with the CENVAT rate by 2006-2007 with two rates, one for service providers to avail credit, and a lower rate for those who do not avail the same.
4. For those service providers with an annual threshold limit up to ₹ 10 lakh, it should be taxed at the rate of 1 percent on the basis of self-assessment without providing input credit for the duty paid on the input goods and services.
5. There should be a comprehensive separate legislation for levy of service tax which should be ultimately integrated with the Central excise law ultimately.
6. Classification of services should be on the lines of World Trade Organization (WTO) classification.
7. Suitable legal provisions should be made for voluntary payment of service tax with provision for automatic collapse of a show cause notice without prosecution if the duty is

voluntarily paid along with an interest and 25 percent penalty within a period of 30 days for early settlement of disputes.

8. A provision similar to that contained in Central Excise Act, 1994 should be provided in respect of non-recovery of service tax in certain situations.
9. Service tax should be introduced as a first e-tax with facility of online filing of returns and payment of tax.

As recommended by Kelkar, a separate comprehensive legislation with unique administrative machinery is very much essential to streamline the tax administration so as to enhance the revenue productivity and improving the culture of voluntary tax compliance. Similarly, on the recommendations of Mr. Kelkar, the Service Directorate proposed an online web-based electronic tax administration system for service tax to provide online registration, payment of tax, filing of returns, assessment, etc. for better tax administration. In its interim report, it opined that such a system can be implemented with least cost and if the system is implemented, it will be the first e-tax and would serve as a model for other tax administrations.

6.9 Constitutional and Legal Issues

Under Article 265 of the Constitution, there was no mention of service tax in any of three categories viz., Union List, State List and Concurrent List under the VII Schedule. However, the Central government used the residuary Entry No. 97 in the Union List for levy of service tax. The Constitutional validity of the service tax has been challenged in various courts across India. But High Courts and the Supreme Court have upheld its validity. The honourable Supreme Court while upholding the validity of the service tax in one of these cases, stated that the imposition of the only levy is on the service provider and not on the customers who are receiving the service and that the charge of tax is on the value of the services and that only the person who provides the service can be regarded as an assessee.

6.10 Revenue Analysis

The service tax revenue has grown gradually and

steadily right since its introduction during the year 1994. Staring from its inception and with just three services, namely, telephones, non-life insurance and stock brokers, and an assessee base of just 4,000, its annual revenue collection was ₹ 410 crore, at a modest tax rate of 5 percent. Over the years, both the revenue and the assessee base has expanded manifold as is evident from Table 6.5.

Table 6.5: Growth of Service Tax Revenue

Year	Revenue (₹ crore)	Percent Growth	No. of Assesses	Percent Growth
1994-95	410	-	3,943	-
1995-96	846	101	4,866	19.0
1996-97	1,022	24	13,982	187.0
1997-98	1,515	49	45,991	228.0
1998-99	1,787	18	1,07,479	133.0
1999-00	2,072	16	1,15,495	7.0
2000-01	2,540	23	1,22,326	6.0
2001-02	3,305	26	1,87,577	53.0
2010-11	58,422	22	13,39,812	9.3
2011-12	71,016	37	14,94,449	11.5
2012-13	97,509	36	16,76,105	12.2
2013-14	1,32,601	17	18,71,939	11.7
2014-15	1,54,780	22	12,76,860	-31.8

Source: Directorate of Service Tax, Mumbai.

The tax rate of 5 percent from 1994-95 to 2002-2003 was replaced with 8 percent from 2004-05 and from 2015-2016, it has been further increased to 14 percent. Even with the tax rate of 5 percent, the growth of revenue and the assessee base has been remarkable over the years with an average growth of 37 percent and 90 percent respectively. The number of services brought under tax net over the years also increased to more than 100 in 2013-14 from just 3 in 1994-95.

But the growth of revenue and assessee base was phenomenal during 2010-2015. One of the reasons for this rapid growth in revenue is the periodic increase in the rate of tax over the years. Even though more than 100 services are under the tax net, only a few services, such as stock brokers, telephone, insurance, advertising, courier, construction engineers, auxiliary services, banking and port services contributing more than ₹ 100 crore in a year had a revenue share of 40 percent among all the services.

However, the revenue realized by the service tax has not been commensurate with the growth of this sector and its contribution to the GDP. The percentage contribution to GDP of service sector had grown from 48 percent in 1994-95 to 60 percent in 2014-15, but its relative share among the taxes was 13.6 percent and in terms of GDP, it was 1.36 percent.

Thus, the service tax has been more responsive to the change in GDP as the volume of revenue realized was 1.36 percent and the share of revenue from services has had a direct relationship with the increase in the share of service sector to the GDP (Table 6.6).

Table 6.6: Share of Service Tax in Total Revenue

Year	Percent Share in Total Revenue	Percentage of GDP	Services Contribution to GDP
1994-95	0.5	0.05	48
1995-96	0.8	0.09	49
1996-97	0.8	0.11	48
1997-98	1.2	0.15	51
1998-99	1.3	0.17	52
1999-00	1.4	0.18	53
2000-01	1.6	0.21	54
2001-02	1.8	0.26	54
2002-03	2.3	0.31	56
2003-04	3.3	0.55	57
2010-11	9.4	0.90	57
2011-12	8.9	0.91	57
2012-13	11.0	1.08	57
2013-14	12.8	1.31	59
2014-15	13.6	1.36	60

Source: National Accounts Statistics, Central Statistical Office, Delhi.

Hence, to evolve an efficient taxation system responsive to the changes in GDP, it is imperative to bring more and more services under the tax net and to give up the selective approach being adopted. It should have a comprehensive approach by taxing all the services barring a small negative list consisting of basic public services and merit goods. Only by bringing all services under the tax net, it is possible to provide relief on input taxes and zero-rating of exports. Moreover, selective approach has administrative disadvantage of defining each service and their ambiguities often leads to litigation with more number of cases pending with the various judicial forums relating to the definition and service of tax on various issues. At the same time, for administrative convenience, it is also necessary to exempt services in the unorganized sector by prescribing a threshold turnover to avoid harassment of small service providers.

6.11 Conclusion

Since service tax is going to be a major source of revenue for the government, a well co-coordinated system of taxation on manufacturing, trade and services without giving room for cascading, would be an ideal system for the future. Therefore, at the central level, service tax should be integrated with CENVAT by taxing all services except a few on the negative list to devise the manufacturing level VAT on both goods and services with a uniform rate of taxation. Since services are intangible, it is difficult to assess the broad base of the sector. At the state level, the service tax should be integrated with the sales tax so as to evolve a harmonized tax system.

However, the states are not empowered to levy taxes on services. Therefore, a Constitutional amendment is necessary to empower the states to levy tax on services so as to enable the states to levy taxes on all tradable services and provide input credits for all input and output taxes paid on services forming inputs in the manufacturing trading of goods and services. Importantly, tax evaders should attract penal provisions without any leniency.

Endnotes

1. Sukumar, Mukhopadhay (2002), "Globalisation and Indian Services Sector", *Economic and Political Weekly*, Mumbai, October 5, 2002, p. 18.
2. Bagchi, Amaresh (1994), "Reform of Domestic Trade Taxes in India: Issues and Options", National Institute of Public Finance and Policy, New Delhi, pp. 10-12.
3. Bagchi, Amaresh (2001), "The Way to Tax Services", *Economic Times*, April 25, 2001.
4. Chelliah, Raja J. (1991), "Tax Reforms Committee", Interim Report, Ministry of Finance, Government of India, New Delhi.
5. Government of India (1994-95), "Budget, 1994-95", speech of the Minister of Finance presenting the Union Government's Budget.
6. Gordon, Jim and Poonam Gupta (2003), "Understanding India's Services Revolution", Paper prepared for the IMF-NCEAR Conference, November 14-16, New Delhi.
7. Virmani, Arvind (2003), "Central Value Added Tax (CENVAT)", Indian Council for Research on International Economic Relations.
8. Kelkar, Vijay (2002), "Task Force on Direct and Indirect Tax Reforms", Ministry of Finance, Government of India.

7

Customs Duties

7.1 Introduction

Customs duty is a tax levied on goods imported into India and on goods exported from India. Under the Constitution, Union Government is empowered to make legislations and collect duties on imports and exports. Customs Act, 1962, is the basic law for levy and collection of customs duty in India. The Central Board of Excise and Customs (CBEC) is the apex body which is a part of the Department of Revenue under the Ministry of Finance which deals with the various functions related to customs. The functions of CBEC are: framing of policies related to levy and collection of customs duties, prevention of smuggling and evasion of duties and all administrative matters. The Board executes its functions through its field organizations namely the Customs, Customs (Preventive) and Central Excise Zones, Commissionerate of Customs, Customs (Preventive), Central Revenues Control Laboratory and Directorates. It also supervises the taxes on foreign and inland travel and ensures the prompt payment by the collection agencies.

7.2 History of Customs Duty

The formation of the Board of Revenue in Calcutta during the year 1786 by the East India Company was the first body to deal with customs duty. Subsequently in 1808, a new Board was launched to deal with all matters related to export and import of goods from India. Later in 1859, Uniform Tariff Act was introduced in lieu of Customs Duties Act and extended to the entire country. In 1878, the erstwhile British Government passed the Sea Customs Act repealing the Uniform Tariff Act announced in 1859.

Afterwards in 1894, Indian Tariff Act was passed replacing the 1859 Act. In 1911, Indian Aircrafts Act was introduced to cover air customs. In 1924, the Land Customs Act was passed. In 1962, the Government of India passed the Customs Act, 1962 replacing the earlier Sea Customs Act and other related legislations. Also, the Customs Tariff Act, 1975 (CTA) was introduced in lieu of Indian Tariff Act passed in 1934.

Conservation of foreign exchange through restriction of imports is the foremost goal of levying customs duties. Safeguarding the interests of domestic industries from undue competition from abroad, achieving the policy objectives of the Government by controlling the imports and exports, regulation of export and co-ordination of laws dealing with Foreign Trade Act, Foreign Exchange Regulation Act, Conservation of Foreign Exchange and Prevention of Smuggling Act etc. are the other important aims of customs duties.

7.3 Types of Customs Duties in India

7.3.1 Basic Customs Duty: Basic customs duty is the tax levied on all goods imported into India under Customs Act, 1962 and it may be fixed as a percentage of the value of the goods or at a specific rate.

7.3.2 Countervailing Duty of Customs: It is an additional duty on goods imported and is equal to the value of imports and excise duty on similar products manufactured in India.

7.3.3 Export Duties: It is a tax levied on all goods exported from India under the Customs Act, 1962. The goods chargeable and the rate of tax are given in the Customs Tariff Act, 1975. However, the Government has emergency powers to change the duty rates and levy fresh export duty depending on the circumstances.

7.3.4 Auxiliary Duty of Customs: This duty is levied under the Finance Act and is imposed on all goods imported into the country at the rate of 50 percent of their value. However, this statutory rate has been reduced in the case of certain types of goods.

7.3.5 Cesses: Cesses are leviable on some specified articles of exports like coffee, coir, lac, mica, tobacco (unmanufactured), marine products, cashew kernels, black pepper, cardamom, iron ore, oil cakes and meals, animal feed and turmeric. These cesses are collected as part of customs duties and are then passed on to the agencies in charge of the administration of the concerned commodities.

7.3.6 Education Cess on Customs Duty: A 2 percentage education cess was imposed on imported goods from July 9, 2004 and further increased to 3 percent of the aggregate duty of customs apart from safeguard duty, countervailing duty and anti-dumping duty.

7.3.7 Protective Duties: Tariff Commission has been established under the Tariff Commission Act, 1951. If the Tariff Commission recommends and Central Government is satisfied that immediate action is necessary to protect interests of the Indian industry, protective customs duty at the rate recommended may be imposed under Section 6 of the Customs Tariff Act. The protective duty will be valid till the date prescribed in the notification.

7.3.8 Countervailing Duty on Subsidized Goods: If a country subsidizes (directly or indirectly) to its exporters for exporting goods to India, the Central Government can impose countervailing duty up to the amount of such subsidy under Section 9 of the Customs Tariff Act.

7.3.9 Anti-dumping Duty: Some manufacturers abroad export huge volume of goods at cheaper rates with the sole aim of damaging the domestic industry which is otherwise called 'dumping'. In order to protect the domestic industry from such anti-dumping, the Central government can impose, under Section 9A of Customs Tariff Act, an anti-dumping duty up to the margin of dumping on such articles, if the goods are being sold at less than its normal value.

7.3.10 Safeguard Duty: To safeguard the domestic industry from the onslaught of exporters abroad, the Central government is empowered to impose a 'safeguard duty' for a limited period if it satisfies that the goods being imported is injurious for the domestic industry.

7.3.11 National Calamity Contingent Duty: A National Calamity Contingent Duty (NCCD) of customs has been imposed on pan masala, chewing tobacco and cigarettes under Section 129 of the Finance Act, 2001 and it varies from 10 percent to 45 percent. NCCD of customs of 1 percent was imposed on polyester filament yarn, motor cars, multi-utility vehicles and two wheelers and NCCD of ₹ 50 per ton was imposed on domestic crude oil, vide Section 134 of the Finance Act, 2003.

There are different rates of duty for different goods imported from certain countries in terms of bilateral or other agreements with such countries which are called preferential rate of duties and the duty may be percentage of the value of the goods or at a specified rate.

7.4 Revenue Importance

Customs duties are a major source of revenue for the Union Government and currently its contribution is nearly 15 percent to the exchequer. Custom duty not only raises money for the Central government but also helps the government to prevent the illegal imports and illegal exports of goods from India. The Central government has emergency powers to increase import or export duties whenever necessary after a notification in the session of the Parliament. Until 1991, the growth rate was remarkable with the contribution touching nearly 40 percent of the gross revenue. Following the introduction of structural reforms in the country in 1991 and a series of reform measures following the recommendations of the Tax Reforms Committee (1991) taken by the Union Government aimed at rationlisation of tax rates, the contribution of customs duty reduced to 15 percent (Table 7.1).

7.5 Mode of Levy

Basically, there are three modes of imposing customs duty:

7.5.1 Ad valorem Duties: Ad valorem custom duty is a duty imposed as a percentage of the total value of a commodity imported or exported. For example, 10 percent of the value of gold imported or 10 percent of gems exported. In case of ad valorem custom duty, the physical units of commodity are not taken into consideration.

7.5.2 Specific Duties: Specific custom duty is a duty imposed on each and every unit of a commodity imported or exported. For example, ₹ 5 on each meter of cloth imported or ₹ 500 on each T.V. set imported.

Table 7.1: Trends of Customs Revenues

Year	Customs Duty (₹ crore)	Contribution (percent)	Percentage to GDP
1950-51	157	39.5	1.6
1960-61	170	19.7	1.0
1970-71	524	16.8	1.1
1980-81	3,409	26.8	2.4
1990-91	20,644	37.0	3.6
2000-01	47,542	25.5	2.3
2001-02	40,268	21.8	1.9
2004-05	57,611	19.0	1.8
2005-06	64,215	17.4	1.5
2006-07	86,327	18.5	2.0
2007-08	1,04,119	17.8	2.1
2008-09	99,879	17.0	1.8
2009-10	83,324	13.6	1.3
2010-11	1,35,813	17.4	1.7
2011-12	1,49,328	17.0	1.7
2012-13	1,64,853	16.0	1.7
2013-14	1,87,308	15.3	1.7
2014-15	1,88,016	15.3	1.9
2015-16	2,09,500	14.5	2.0

Source: Budget Documents, Ministry of Finance, Government of India.

7.5.3 Compound Duties: Compound custom duty is the

combination of specific and ad valorem custom duties. In this case, the quantities as well as the value of the commodity are taken into consideration while computing tariff. For example, 5 percent of value plus 50 paisa per meter of cloth imported.

7.6 Harmonization of Customs Duty

During 1980s, the tariff rates were very high and the duty structure was complex. The Long Term Fiscal Policy (LTFP) announced by the Government in 1985-86 stressed the need for gradual reduction of tariff rates, imposing uniform tax rates and elimination of quantitative restrictions on imports. Subsequently, rationalization of tariff rates was carried out for specific industries such as capital goods, drug intermediates, and electronic goods. In spite of these rationalization measures, in 1989-90, the weighted average tariff rate was 87 percent compared to 38 percent in 1980-81. By 1990-91, the tariff structure ranged from 0 to 400 percent due to various reasons such as exemptions, political lobbying, revenue mobilization, etc. and led to a more complicating system of tax collection.

Customs duties have been utilized for safeguarding the local industries against the onslaught of industries abroad and conservation of foreign exchange, besides, being an important source of revenue for the Government. After Independence, the Government under the guise of regulating trade, effected various non-tariff policies, which landed customs duties into a trap of license raj and higher tariff rates. It was only after the recommendations of the Tax Reforms Committee (TRC) in 1991, the Government deregulated trade and abolished licensing procedures in tandem with globalization of the Indian economy.

Tax Reforms Committee (1991) made three recommendations to rationalize India's customs tariff rates. The recommendations were as under:

- A reduction in the general level of tariffs.
- A reduction in the dispersion of tariff rates.

- Elimination of innumerable exemptions and concessions.

Accepting the recommendations of the TRC, the Union Government in 1991 reduced the peak duty rate from 300 percent to 150 percent. In 1992, it was reduced to 110 percent and then to 85 percent in 1993-1994. During 1994-1995 and 1995-1996, the peak rate was further reduced to 65 percent and 50 percent respectively. In 1994, the Union Government eliminated the end-use based exemptions. The current peak rate of duty is 10 percent on non-agricultural items (except for natural rubber sheets, fish and cars). The average import tariff and the dispersion in duty rates have been falling since 1991.

The downward momentum was reversed the next year with the imposition of a surcharge. This momentum has resumed with the reduction of the "peak" rate to 35 percent in 2001-02 and 30 percent in 2002-03. In 2003-04, peak rate of customs duty was reduced from 30 percent to 25 percent excluding agricultural and dairy products. The peak customs duty was lowered to 10 percent from 12.5 percent in the Budget for 2007-08 and it has been retained till 2015-16.

7.7 Comparison of Customs Revenue between Pre- and Post-reforms Period

The responsiveness of tax revenues to discretionary changes in the tax rate and in the tax base in relation to the GDP is termed the buoyancy of the tax system and is expressed as:

$$B= (\Delta T/\Delta Y) \times(Y/T))*100$$

where

B = buoyancy of tax revenue to GDP

T = total tax revenue

Y = GDP

ΔT = change in total tax revenue

ΔY = change in GDP

Annual Average Growth Rate (AAGR) = average year to year growth rate over a period of time.

Revenue Stability: A simple measure of the stability of

tax revenue is the coefficient of variation (CV), which is defined as the standard deviation of tax revenue (as a fraction of GDP usually) divided by its mean.

Coefficient of Variation = Standard Deviation + Mean.

Due to the implementation of tax reforms from 1991-92, the buoyancy of customs revenues has fallen from 1.49 percent to 0.79 percent compared to the pre-reforms period. But the exports have risen to 9.22 percent from 5.38 percent during the post-reforms period (Table 7.2).

The AAGR has almost reduced to 50 percent (4 percent) during the post-reforms period compared to the pre-reforms period (8 percent). The AAGR for exports has improved to 18.36 percent from 16.44 percent compared to the pre-reforms period.

The customs revenue has been more volatile (7.4 percent) during the post-reforms period than the pre-reforms period (6.2 percent). But the exports recorded a stable growth (55 percent) during the post-reforms period compared to the pre-reforms period (69.77 percent).

Table 7.2: Comparison of Customs Revenue and Export Performance

	Customs Revenue		**Export Performance**	
	Pre-Reforms Period	Post-Reforms Period	Pre-Reforms Period	Post-Reforms Period
Buoyancy (percent)	1.49	0.76	5.38	9.22
AAGR (percent)	8.00	4.00	16.44	18.36
C.V.	6.20	7.40	69.77	55.15

7.8 Conclusion

Substantial progress has been made in harmonizing the customs duty structure to facilitate Indian industries to have a competitive edge in the global market. Reduction in tariffs, simplification of procedures and abolition of end use exemptions can be hailed as important milestones in the harmonization of customs duties in India.

8

Towards National Level Goods and Services Tax (GST)

8.1 Introduction

The successful implementation of value added tax (VAT) in 2005 by the States is hailed as one of the boldest innovative tax reform undertaken in independent India. The design of VAT implemented was based on a study "Reform of Domestic Trade Taxes in India: Issues and Options" done by Late Dr. Amaresh Bagchi. Considering the fragile nature of the Centre-State financial relations, the study recommended a dual VAT: a Central VAT replacing the existing Central excise duty and a State VAT replacing the existing sales tax system in the States. The Report also clearly spelt out that dual VAT recommendation is only a short-term and feasible solution to the complex taxation system in India and the immediate implementation may pave the way for a more progressive, rational, destination-based consumption type taxation system covering both goods and services in future.

8.2 Deficiencies of the Dual VAT System in India

8.2.1 Exclusion of Services: A study done by the National Institute of Public Finance and Policy in 1994 pointed out that services often become an integral part of manufacturing and trade and the line between goods and services is getting increasingly blurred as for instance, development of software, desktop publishing, printing of photographs, etc. which involves a variety of services such as training, installation and maintenance. By taking advantage of these definitional ambiguities, the manufacturers in collusion with the traders underestimate the value of manufactured goods by claiming discounts for post-manufacturing services such as transportation, installation and maintenance.

In case of sales taxes too, the first point taxation on goods where the base is free of services and trade margins tend to distort consumers and producers as items which carry higher trade margins are more favoured than the essential goods and the producers add more number of services to underestimate the value of their products. This shortcoming may be viewed in two different aspects. Basically, the development of information technology has distorted the distinction between goods and services. Even though goods are defined to include intangibles such as copyright and software, these are often supplied as a service contract.

Also, value added services supplied in addition to telecommunication services such as news alerts, ring tones, scores of games, weather reports, etc.; are some which could be considered as goods. In our daily life, goods and services are often offered as composite bundles. Under the present system of taxation, only parts of the bundle alone can be taxed. The state governments, though they are not empowered to levy taxes on services, stretching beyond their powers, have imposed multiple levies such as luxury tax on hotels and restaurants, betting tax, lottery tax, entertainment tax, electricity duty, taxes on passengers and goods, etc. to increase their revenue. When VAT is introduced by merging the services and goods, these multiple levies become a part and parcel of the VAT and the tax system will become simple. Hence, not only from the point of view of improving the revenue productivity, but also from evolving an efficient, systematic and orderly taxation system without distortions, taxing services along with the goods becomes necessary.

8.2.2 Tax Cascading: The coverage of commodities under CENVAT is not comprehensive as certain sectors such as oil and gas production, agriculture, wholesale and retail trade, real estate and construction remain outside the scope of CENVAT and service taxes. These sectors cannot claim any input tax credit (ITC) under CENVAT and service tax. Under State VAT too, ITCs are not allowed for service sector, real estate properties, agriculture etc.

As central sales tax (CST) levied on inter-State trade, being an origin-based tax is inconsistent with destination-based taxes such as VAT where input tax credit is permitted. In an apparent move towards introducing GST, the rate of central sales tax for inter-State trade was reduced from 4 percent to 3 percent with effect from April 1, 2007 and further reduced to 2 percent from June 1, 2008. Central sales tax on inter-State trade is the most contributing factor to tax cascading as the tax is collected by the exporting state for which no ITC is permitted. Consequently, the extent of tax cascading is huge under CENVAT, service tax and the state VAT on account of the innumerable exemptions and restricted ITC claims.

Tax cascading puts the domestic producers in a most disadvantageous position in the global market. The burden of hidden taxes along with the statutory tax rates increases the cost of domestic production activities and creates conducive environment for imports which do not bear any hidden taxes. In such cascading system of taxes, most governments fail to bring any intended changes in the overall economy of the state.

Over the years, many commodities were exempted from CENVAT and the tax rate also reduced for specific commodities which are politically sensitive. Similarly, service tax coverage is incremental and imposed only on select services.

8.2.3 Demerits of State VAT: The distinction between goods and services as defined in the Constitution is highly confused and not in accordance with the realities of modern economies. Constitution defines 'goods' as tangible and movable. Services form an integral part of manufacturing and trade such as computer software development, desktop publishing, developers (manufacturers) providing training, installation and maintenance apart from the supply of the software. Therefore, exclusion of services from manufacturing and trade base and the failure of the Central government to extend taxation beyond manufacturing and trade reduce the assessable value of goods artificially low and create confusion as to what constitutes the 'sale of goods'. States are not empowered to tax services. Hence, during contingencies, states which have no other alternative source of revenue resort to setting tax rates beyond the floor rates.

Another shortcoming is the non-application of floor rates in some states where some items have been brought down from 12.5 percent to 4 percent and some commodities from 4 percent to 0 percent resulting in wide variation and thereby defeating the very purpose of setting the floor rates. This diversion of trade goes against the principle of tax harmonization. The application of VAT on MRP (maximum retail price) at the first point on drugs in West Bengal and Maharashtra goes against the principle of VAT, as there would be no addition of value at the subsequent stages. The wide variation of 8.5 percent between the tax rates of inputs and output (4 percent and 12.5 percent) may result in revenue loss for the government, as many commodities are used as inputs as well as outputs and the manufacturers are tempted to suppress the sale of output and prefer to pay 4 percent on inputs. The wide variation towards the tax rates of inputs and outputs may encourage lobbying to cover more number of such commodities in future.

8.3 Service Tax Growth in India

Initially, when service tax was introduced in 1994, only three services (telephones, non-life insurance and stock brokers) were taxed under the Finance Act, 1994. Subsequently, under Finance Acts of 1996, 1997, 1998, 2001, 2002 and 2003, additional services were added and the total number of services went up to 58 and four services such as goods transport operators, outdoor caterers, *pandal* and *shamiyana* contractors, *mandap* keepers and mechanized slaughter houses were excluded from tax from 1997-98. Since its inception in 1994-95, service tax collections have grown from ₹ 407 crore in 1994-95 to ₹ 2,10,000 crore in 2015-16. The share of service tax has increased from 0.44 per cent in 1994-95 to 14.5 percent in 2015-16. The growth of service tax over the years has been volatile due to the additional coverage of services and exemptions.

Having recognized the revenue potential of the service sector, the government appointed a Committee under the chairmanship of former Revenue Secretary Dr. Vijay Kelkar to suggest ways for the overall improvement of service taxation in India. The Committee recommended the following.

1. Service tax should be levied comprehensively leaving out a specific negative list of exempted and merit goods.
2. Integration of both CENVAT credit and service tax credits.
3. The rate of service tax should achieve parity with the CENVAT rate by 2006-2007 with two rates, one for service providers availing credit, and a lower rate for those who do not avail credit.
4. For those service providers with an annual threshold limit up to ₹ 10 lakh they should be taxed at a rate of 1 percent on the basis of self-assessment without providing input credit of the duty paid on the input goods and services.
5. There should be a comprehensive separate legislation for levy of service tax which should ultimately be integrated with the Central Excise Law ultimately.
6. Classification of services should be on the lines of World Trade Organization classification.
7. Suitable legal provisions should be made for voluntary payment of service tax with provision for automatic collapse of a show cause notice without prosecution if the duty is voluntariiy paid along with the interest and 25 percent penalty within a period of 30 days for early settlement of disputes.
8. A provision similar to that contained in Central Excise Act, 1994 should be provided in respect of non-recovery of service tax in certain situations.
9. Service tax should be introduced as a first e-tax with the facility on online filing of returns and payment of tax.

8.4 Goods and Services Tax

To overcome the above mentioned deficiencies in the CENVAT and State VAT dispensations, the Union Finance Minister while presenting the Union Budget for 2006-2007, announced that goods and service tax (GST) would be implemented from April 11, 2010. The Empowered Committee of State Finance Ministers has been holding deliberations to prepare a roadmap for the implementation of the GST. Due to various reasons, the implementation of GST has been delayed.

8.4.1 History of GST: The concept of goods and services tax was first conceived by the French taxman Apparatchik Maurice Lauré in 1954. So far more than 160 countries have introduced GST in one or the other form including the European Union and Asian countries such as Sri Lanka, Singapore and China. In most of the countries, GST has been introduced as a unified system (Table 8.1).

Table 8.1: Introduction of GST in Various Countries

Country	Year of Introduction	Rate of GST (percent)
Australia	2000	10.0
France	1954	19.6
China	1980	5.0
United Kingdom	1994	17.5
Thailand	1991	7.0
Singapore	1994	5.0
New Zealand	1985	12.5

8.4.2 GST in India: The Constitution Amendment Bill 2014 (122nd Amendment) introduced by the Finance Minister on December, 19, 2014 envisages the following:

1. Towards achieving a common market in India by removing barriers in the form of cascading effects of taxation, the Central Government introduced the 122nd Constitution Amendment Bill, 2014 on the introduction of

goods and services tax (GST).

2. The Bill proposes to replace the existing multi-tiered Indian taxation system. Currently, the Centre imposes excise duty on manufacture of goods, and service tax on select services apart from customs duty on imports. The States levy value added tax (VAT) on the supply of goods and a plethora of taxes such as entertainment tax, excise duties on alcohol and medicinal and toilet preparations (MTP), entry tax and octroi. For mixed supply of services and goods, some activities such as construction, restaurants, etc., both service tax and VAT apply on the respective components. This results in a multiplicity of taxes with limited cross credits, conceptual difficulties, differential tax regimes between States and undue litigation.
3. The Bill proposes that both the Centre and States would have concurrent powers to levy GST on the supply of goods and services within a State. In reality, every supply of goods and services would attract a Central GST (CGST) and a State GST (SGST) on a common base.
4. For inter-State trade, a levy called integrated goods and services tax (IGST) would be levied by the Centre. IGST revenues would be shared between the Centre and States as per the recommendations of the GST Council.
5. Imports to be treated at par with inter-State transactions and therefore should attract IGST.
6. GST would be levied on the sale of newspapers and advertisements therein.
7. Stamp duties, typically imposed on legal agreements by the State, would continue to be levied by the States.
8. The Bill has provided for a definition of services, as "anything other than goods", which is based on the system prevalent under the VAT regimes in the European Union.
9. The Bill provides that the administration of GST would be the responsibility of the GST Council which would then become the apex indirect tax policy making body of the

country. This GST Council would be formed by the Central and State level ministers in charge of the finance portfolio. The Bill also lays down various elements of how the GST Council would operate and its powers, such as determining the rate and exemptions of tax, threshold limits, framing model laws and principles of levy and apportionment of IGST, and voting powers.

10. The bill proposes to subsume the following taxes under the Central goods and service tax (CGST).

- Central excise duty.
- Additional service duties.
- Excise Duty on Medicinal and Toilet Preparation Act, 1955.
- Service tax.
- Additional customs duty [countervailing Duty (CVD)].
- Special additional duty of custom.
- Central surcharges and Cesses.

Under the State goods and services tax (SGST), the following taxes are subsumed.

- State VAT.
- Central sales tax.
- Luxury tax.
- Entry tax (other than those in lieu of octroi).
- Entertainment tax (not levied by the local bodies).
- Taxes on advertisements.
- Taxes on lotteries, betting and gambling.
- State cesses and surcharges insofar as they relate to supply of goods or services.

11. Credit of CGST paid on inputs may be used only for paying CGST on the output and the credit of SGST paid on inputs may be used only for paying SGST. In other words, no cross input credits are permitted.
12. Tobacco and tobacco products would be subject to GST. Also, the Centre could continue to levy Central excise duty and the States to levy sales tax/VAT.
13. A common threshold exemption would apply to both

CGST and SGST. Dealers with a turnover below it would be exempt from tax. A compounding option (i.e. to pay tax at a flat rate without credits) would be available to small dealers below a certain threshold. The threshold exemption and compounding provision would be optional.

14. The list of exempted goods and services would be kept to a minimum and it would be harmonized for the Centre and the States as far as possible.
15. Exports would be zero-rated.
16. The integrated GST (IGST) on inter-State supply of goods or services would be collected by the Centre so that the credit chain is not disrupted. Accounts would be settled periodically between the Centre and the States to ensure that the SGST used for payment of IGST is transferred to the destination State where the goods or services are ultimately consumed.

Under the dual system of GST, the states are empowered to levy GST besides central GST on a common base from the production point to the final consumption. Hence, states have much broader tax base under the GST regime. Currently, the Union government alone is empowered to tax services and goods up to the production stage whereas the state governments are empowered for levying sales tax on the goods sold within its territory. Imports are charged with custom duty by the Union government while states charge sales tax on them. Under the GST regime, states will be empowered to tax not only the goods but the services as well as the imports. Constitution Amendment Bill, 2014 seeks to empower both the States and the Union Government to have concurrent power to levy GST on goods, services and imports at all levels. The main goal is to have a broader tax base with lower tax rates to mitigate the cascading effects of taxes and remove hidden taxes from exports to make them globally competitive. The taxpayers will have a common registration throughout the country and would be required to file returns both with the States and the Centre so as to improve tax compliance and tax revenues. Tax administration will become easier as most of the levies are going to be subsumed under the GST.

8.5 Computation of GST

Suppose a textile spinning mill purchases cotton from a cotton dealer at a cost of ₹ 100. The spinning mill made yarn and supplied it to a weaver at a cost of ₹ 150. The weaver in turn supplied cloth at a cost of ₹ 200 to a wholesaler who in turn sold it to the retailer at a cost of ₹ 300. Finally, the retailer sold it to the consumer at a cost of ₹ 400. Assuming a GST tax rate of 10 percent, Table 8.2 would provide an idea of GST computation for the same.

The total GST liability would be ₹ 40.

Table 8.2: GST Computation

Supplier/ Manufacturer (1)	Cost of Input (₹) (2)	Value of Goods and Services Output (₹) (3)	Value Addition (₹) (4)
Cotton Supplier	-	100	0
Spinner	100	150	50
Weaver	150	200	50
Wholesaler	200	300	100
Retailer	300	400	100

Contd...

GST of 10 Percent on Output (₹) (5)	Input Tax Credit (₹) (6)	Net GST (₹) (5 - 6) (7)
10	-	10
15	10	5 = 15-10
20	15	5 = 20-15
30	20	10 = 30-20
40	30	10 = 40-30

8.5.1 Operationalization of SGST, CGST and IGST: Let us assume a rate of tax under CGST and SGST at 10 percent. When a manufacturer of grinders in Tamil Nadu sells grinders to a wholesaler in Tamil Nadu for ₹ 500, the manufacturer would charge CGST of ₹ 50 and SGST of ₹ 50 besides the basic price of the goods. The manufacturer is required to pay the CGST charge of ₹ 50 into a Central Government account and SGST charge of ₹ 50 into the account of Tamil Nadu government. In case if the manufacturer had paid CGST and SGST for the inputs, he is entitled to set-off for his CGST or SGST paid on his inputs. Suppose if the value of the input purchased is ₹ 100, the input tax credit would be ₹ 10 each for CGST and SGST. The manufacturer is supposed to pay a net GST of ₹ 40 (₹ 50-₹ 10) after deducting the CGST credit. But for paying CGST, he is entitled to use only the credit of CGST paid on his purchases and for SGST he can utilize the credit of SGST alone. In other words, cross utilisation of CGST credit is not permitted for payment of SGST.

8.5.2 Inter-State Transactions (Integrated Goods and Services Tax): Let us assume a CGST and the SGST of 10 percent. Consequently, the IGST would be 20 percent (SGST + CGST). Suppose a dealer 'X' in Tamil Nadu purchases goods worth ₹ 1,000 and sells goods to dealer 'Y' in Karnataka at ₹ 2,000. Assuming that the credit available under CGST and SGST is ₹ 100 each, the tax payable on inter-State sales would be ₹ 400. Dealer 'X' would have to maintain two invoices. In one invoice, input tax credits on the purchase of inputs (i.e. CGST of ₹ 100 and SGST of ₹ 100) and in the other invoice payment for the inter-State transaction (₹ 400) to Tamil Nadu government have to be maintained. The state of Tamil Nadu collects the tax and transfers it to the Centre. As dealer X is entitled to claim input tax credits, the actual tax to be paid would be ₹ 200 [₹ 400-₹ 100 (CGST)-₹ 100 (SGST)]. Now it is ensured that the entire tax revenue of ₹ 400 (₹ 100 for Centre (CGST) + ₹ 100 transferred by State to the Centre + ₹ 200 for IGST paid by dealer X) is transferred to the Centre. The importing dealer Y will claim credit of IGST while clearing his output tax liability in Karnataka. The Centre will transfer to the Karnataka, the credit of IGST used in payment of SGST. The appropriate information is submitted to the Central government which acts as a clearing house mechanism, to verify the claims and intimate the concerned state governments to transfer the funds.

8.5.3 Illustration of Computing GST: A manufacturer purchased inputs for ₹ 1,00,000 and incurred a production cost (services) of ₹ 5,000. These manufactured goods were sold for ₹ 1,50,000. The CGST and SGST rates are 10 percent and 12 percent respectively. The tax liability and the value of final good would be as shown in Table 8.3.

Table 8.3: Computation of Tax Liability and the Value of Final Good

Particulars	Amount (₹)
Cost of inputs	1,00,000
Production cost	5,000
Profit margin	20,000
Sales	1,25,000
CGST: 1,25,000 @ 10 percent	12,500
SGST: 1,25,000 @ 12 percent	15,000
Value of the final good	1,52,500

A. Inter-State Trade GST (IGST): A manufacturer purchases inputs for ₹ 2,00,000 and incurred a production cost of ₹ 30,000. The output was sold for ₹ 3,00,000 to a dealer outside the state. Rate of SGST and CGST is 10 percent each (Table 8.4).

Table 8.4: Computation of Inter-State Trade GST (IGST)

Particulars	Amount (₹)
Cost of inputs	2,00,000
Production cost	30,000
Profit margin	15,000
Sales	2,45,000
IGST: 2,45,000 @ 20 percent (CGST, SGST: 10 percent)	49,000
Sales price	2,94,000

7.5.4 GST in a Supply Chain: With a GST rate of 10 percent, the calculations will be as shown in Table 8.5.

Table 8.5: GST in a Supply Chain

Stage of Supply Chain	Purchase Value of Input (₹)	Value Addition (₹)	Value of Supply (₹)	Rate of GST (percent)
Manufacturer	1,000	300	1,300	10 percent
Wholesaler	1,300	200	1,500	10 percent
Retailer	1,500	100	1,600	10 percent

Contd...

Stage of Supply Chain	GST on Output (₹)	Input Tax Credit (ITC) (₹)	Net GST = GST on Output – ITC (₹)
Manufacturer	130	100	130-100 = 30
Wholesaler	150	130	150-130 = 20
Retailer	160	150	160-150 = 10

A. Manufacturer: A manufacturer makes a value addition of ₹ 300 on inputs and services worth ₹ 100. The manufacturer will then pay a net GST of ₹ 30 after setting-off ₹ 100 as GST paid on his inputs from gross GST of ₹ 130. The manufacturer sells the goods to the wholesaler.

B. Wholesaler: When the wholesaler sells the same goods after making value addition of ₹ 200, he pays a net GST of only ₹ 20, after setting-off input tax credit of ₹ 130 from the gross GST of ₹ 150 to the manufacturer.

C. Retailer: When a retailer sells the same goods after a value addition of ₹ 100, he pays a net GST of only ₹ 10, after setting-off ₹ 150 from his gross GST of ₹ 160 paid to the wholesaler. Thus, the manufacturer, wholesaler and retailer have to pay only ₹ 60 (i.e. ₹ 30 + ₹ 20 + ₹ 10) as GST on the value addition along the entire value chain from the producer to the retailer, after setting-off GST paid at the earlier stages. The final price paid by consumer is ₹ 1,600 + 10 percent of ₹ 1,600 = ₹ 1,760.

8.5.5 Comparison of GST with the Existing Taxes: It is as shown in Table 8.6.

Table 8.6: Comparison of GST with the Existing Taxes

Particulars	Under Existing Taxes (₹)	Under GST (₹)
Manufacture to Wholesaler		
Cost of production (inputs + services)	5,000.00	5,000.00
Profit margin (value addition)	2,000.00	2,000.00
Ex-factory price	7,000.00	7,000.00
Cenvat @ 16 percent	1,120.00	–
Total Value	**8,120.00**	**7,000.00**
VAT @ 12.5 percent	1,015.00	–
CGST @ 5 percent	–	350.00
SGST @ 7 percent	–	490.00
Bill Value	**9,135.00**	**7,840.00**
Cost Saving		**1,295.00**
Wholesaler to Retailer		
Sale to wholesaler	9,135.00	7,840.00
Profit margin	2,000.00	2,000.00
Total value	**11,135.00**	**9,840.00**
VAT @ 12.5 percent	1,392	–
CGST @ 5 percent	–	492.00
SGST @ 7 percent	–	689.00
Input tax credit	377 = 1,392-1,015	341 = 1,181-840
Bill value	11,512.00	10,181.00
Cost saving		1331
Retailer to Consumer		
Sale to retailer	11,512.00	10,181.00
Profit margin	1,000.00	1,000.00
Total Value	12,512.00	11,181.00
VAT @ 12.5 percent	1,564.00	
CGST @ 5 percent	–	559.05
SGST @ 7 percent	–	782.67
Input tax credit	1,187 = 1,564-377	1,000 = 1341-341
Total Price to the Final consumer	13,699.00	12,181.72
Cost saving to consumer	–	**1,041.00**
Total Tax Paid	3,699.00	2,181.00

8.5.6 Treatment of Imports: A manufacturer imported inputs worth of ₹ 20,000 and incurred production cost of ₹ 2,000 to produce final output of goods. Basic customs duty at 10 percent was leviable on imported goods. The manufactured goods were sold within the state at a rate of ₹ 50,000 plus applicable GST. Rate of CGST and SGST is 6 percent and 8 percent respectively.

A. Computation of Net Cost of Imported Goods: It is as shown in Table 8.7.

Table 8.7: Computation of Net Cost of Imported Goods

Particulars	Amount (₹)
Cost of goods imported	20,000
Basic customs duty at 10 percent	2,000
Cost of imported goods (including BCD)	22,000
CGST on import @ 6 percent	1,320
SGST on import @ 8 percent	1,760
Cost of imported goods	25,080

GST is payable before the goods are released.

B. Computation of Sale Value after Import: It is as shown in Table 8.8.

Table 8.8: Computation of Sale Value after Import

Particulars	Amount (₹)
Sale value (before tax)	45,000
CGST on import @ 6 percent	2,700
SGST on import @ 8 percent	3,600
Sale value	50,300

C. Computation of Net GST: It is as shown in Table 8.9.

Table 8.9: Computation of Net GST

Particulars	CGST (₹)	SGST (₹)
Output tax	2,700	3,600
Less: Input tax credit	–	–
CGST	1,320	–
SGST	–	1,760
Net GST	1,380	1,840

8.5.7 Computation of Export Value: Let us suppose that a good worth ₹ 20,000 is exported after a lapse of one year of use after adding a profit margin ₹ 5,000 and the use factor of 1 year for refund calculation is 0.20. Therefore, the refund will be 0.80 of the duty amount.

A. Treatment of Exports: It is as shown in Table 8.10.

Table 8.10: Treatment of Exports

Particulars	Amount (₹)
Cost of imported goods	25,080
Profit margin	5,000
Sale value	30,080
CGST on export @ 5 percent	–
SGST on export @ 7 percent	–
Export value	30,080

B. Refund Calculation: It is as shown in Table 8.11.

Table 8.11: Refund Calculation

Particulars	Amount (₹)
Basic customs duty (BCD, from above example)	2,000
Refund factor	0.80
Refund amount of BDC	1,600
CGST	1,380
SGST	1,840
Total refund amount	6,820

8.6 Computation of Revenue Neutral Rate (RNR) and Estimated Revenues for Major States

To compute the RNR for the States, revenue due to VAT commodities, CST revenue, surcharges, turnover taxes, entertainment taxes, luxury taxes and entry taxes for the last five years (2010-11 to 2014-15) was collected as these taxes are likely to be subsumed under the SGST and projections for the period 2015-16 to 2019-20 have been made. Similarly, net state domestic product (NSDP) at factor cost at current prices was collected for the 22 states and the share of agriculture and allied sector and unregistered manufacturing was subtracted, as more than 95 percent of these sectors remain unorganized. Further, a reduction of 15 percent was made for major manufacturing states as 77 percent of the GSDP of the trade and hotels and restaurants remains in the informal sector in these states and the resultant NSDP has been projected for the period 2016-17 to 2019-20. Revenue neutral rates (RNR) and estimated revenues are presented in Tables 8.12 and 8.13.

Table 8.12: Revenue Neutral Rates (Percent) for State Goods and Services Tax

States	**With CST**			
	2016-17	2017-18	2018-19	2019-20
Andhra Pradesh	9.4	9.9	10.5	11.1
Bihar	4.6	5.6	6.8	8.3
Chhattisgarh	6.2	6.5	7.0	7.4
Goa	5.1	5.5	5.8	6.2
Gujarat	7.7	8.2	8.8	9.4
Haryana	8.5	9.4	10.4	11.5
Jharkhand	5.6	5.8	6.0	6.3
Karnataka	6.6	6.9	7.3	7.7
Kerala	7.0	7.6	8.2	8.9
Madhya Pradesh	5.4	5.9	6.4	6.9
Maharashtra	5.0	5.2	5.4	5.5
Odisha	5.9	6.3	6.7	7.2
Punjab	8.2	8.9	9.6	10.4
Rajasthan	5.8	6.1	6.5	6.8
Tamil Nadu	7.0	7.5	8.0	8.6
Uttar Pradesh	8.1	8.4	8.7	9.0
West Bengal	6.5	7.1	7.7	8.4
Assam	6.7	7.3	8.0	8.7
Himachal Pradesh	6.7	7.3	8.0	8.7
Jammu and Kashmir	10.7	11.8	13.1	14.4
Uttarakhand	8.6	9.2	9.8	10.5
NCT Delhi	5.5	5.7	5.8	5.9
National Average	**7.4**	**7.9**	**8.5**	**7.4**

Contd...

States	Without CST			
	2016-17	2017-18	2018-19	2019-20
Andhra Pradesh	8.9	9.5	10.0	10.6
Bihar	4.5	5.5	6.7	8.2
Chhattisgarh	4.8	5.1	5.4	5.7
Goa	4.7	5.0	5.3	5.7
Gujarat	6.5	7.0	7.5	8.1
Haryana	7.7	8.5	9.4	10.4
Jharkhand	4.6	4.7	4.9	5.1
Karnataka	6.2	6.6	6.9	7.3
Kerala	6.9	7.4	8.0	8.7
Madhya Pradesh	5.0	5.4	5.9	6.4
Maharashtra	4.5	4.7	4.8	5.0
Odisha	5.3	5.7	6.1	6.5
Punjab	7.9	8.6	9.3	10.0
Rajasthan	5.3	5.6	5.9	6.3
Tamil Nadu	6.3	6.8	7.3	7.8
Uttar Pradesh	7.2	7.5	7.7	8.0
West Bengal	5.8	6.3	6.9	7.4
Assam	5.9	6.4	7.0	7.6
Himachal Pradesh	5.9	6.4	7.0	7.6
Jammu and Kashmir	10.0	11.0	12.2	13.4
Uttarakhand	8.6	9.2	9.8	10.5
NCT Delhi	4.9	5.0	5.1	5.3
National Average	**6.3**	**6.8**	**7.3**	**7.9**

8.7 Roadmap for the Introduction of GST

1. Computerisation of all States with end-to-end integration of offices, check-posts and commissionerates using the GST Network developed by the National Securities Depository Ltd. (NSDL) to capture all the inter- and intra-State transactions of goods and services. It is the backbone for implementation of the GST and would be helpful in monitoring transactions and conducting effective verification of returns to detect evasion.
2. Mandatory e-filing of tax returns to ensure instant collection and distribution of tax information to State and Central Governments, so as to ensure cross-verification of the returns which in turn avoids pilferages and fraud in tax collection.
3. The tax return may be designed as simple as possible as the one prescribed by the Thirteenth Finance Commission,

so as to reduce the cost of compliance for the assesses and ensure collection of all basic information for cross-verification to establish the trail of transactions leading to input tax credit (ITC) claims.

4. The software may be developed in such a way that all basic processes, viz., filing of returns, registration, etc., may be standardized across the country and enable non-intrusive and system-based verification of returns, detecting dormant or non-filers and selection of samples for tax audit.
5. The GST Act must specify a timeframe for processing ITC claims and refunds to enhance the confidence of tax payers and binding the tax administration for efficient service delivery.

Table 8.13: Estimated Revenue for States under Goods and Services Tax (in ₹ crore)

States	**With CST**			
	2016-17	2017-18	2018-19	2019-20
Andhra Pradesh	57,849	72,965	92,033	11,6083
Bihar	13,023	17,297	22,974	30,514
Chhattisgarh	10,140	12,125	14,500	17,340
Goa	2,923	3,587	4,402	5,403
Gujarat	56,333	68,859	84,170	1,02,885
Haryana	34,426	43,802	55,732	70,911
Jharkhand	8,938	10,298	11,865	13,671
Karnataka	40,493	48,471	58,021	69,454
Kerala	30,191	37,057	45,485	55,829
Madhya Pradesh	18,564	22,672	27,690	33,818
Maharashtra	64,002	74,614	86,985	1,01,408
Odisha	14,547	17,564	21,206	25,604
Punjab	20,945	25,362	30,711	37,188
Rajasthan	27,043	32,668	39,461	47,668
Tamil Nadu	55,687	67,851	82,670	1,00,727
Uttar Pradesh	43,581	50,533	58,595	67,942
West Bengal	30,766	38,016	46,974	58,044
Assam	8,663	10,510	12,751	15,470
Himachal Pradesh	6,715	8,415	10,546	13,216
Jammu and Kashmir	5,767	6,940	8,352	10,051
Uttarakhand	5,744	6,744	7,919	9,299
NCT Delhi	23,226	26,921	31,204	36,167

Contd...

States	Without CST			
	2016-17	2017-18	2018-19	2019-20
Andhra Pradesh	53,237	64,427	77,944	94,313
Bihar	12,891	17,121	22,740	30,204
Chhattisgarh	7,838	9,373	11,209	13,404
Goa	2,681	3,290	4,038	4,955
Gujarat	48,132	58,834	71,916	87,907
Haryana	31,247	39,758	50,586	64,364
Jharkhand	7,253	8,357	9,629	11,094
Karnataka	38,343	45,898	54,942	65,767
Kerala	29,500	36,209	44,443	54,550
Madhya Pradesh	17,072	20,850	25,465	31,100
Maharashtra	57,687	67,251	78,402	91,401
Odisha	13,206	15,945	19,252	23,245
Punjab	20,112	24,354	29,490	35,710
Rajasthan	24,716	29,856	36,065	43,566
Tamil Nadu	50,581	61,629	75,090	91,491
Uttar Pradesh	38,981	45,199	52,410	60,770
West Bengal	27,400	33,857	41,835	51,693
Assam	7,605	9,227	11,195	13,582
Himachal Pradesh	6,259	7,843	9,828	12,317
Jammu and Kashmir	5,767	6,940	8,352	10,051
Uttarakhand	5,123	6,016	7,064	8,294
NCT Delhi	20,336	23,571	27,321	31,667

6. Capacity building for the staff with due emphasis on the whole gamut of tax processes and handling of these processes through computers may be taken up.
7. Preparation of departmental manuals for standardizing the tax processes may be taken up as it provides a reference point to navigate the GST, organizing training and lays down a framework of internal controls for effective monitoring.
8. Decision on the periodicity of filing returns may be taken in accordance with the turnover of the dealers to reduce the burden on the department and for easy monitoring.
9. Establishment of an independent audit wing is necessary to audit a representative sample of dealers selected on the basis of a scientific risk analysis and completion of audits in time may be initiated.
10. The GST Act should specify the penalty across different types of offences and should provide no room for manipulation.

11. Establishment of a monitoring wing to monitor the entire process and report any deviation in GST implementation in order to take immediate remedial measures.

8.8 Conclusion

The successful implementation of value added tax (VAT) in 2005 by the States is hailed as one of the boldest innovative tax reform taken in independent India. In spite of having problems such as exclusion of services, tax cascading, non-adherence to floor rates, etc., VAT has been successful in most of the Indian States. This gain in performance of State VAT may be taken as a green signal for the transition to the introduction of goods and services tax (GST). In this regard, an attempt is made to estimate the expected revenues and the revenue neutral rates (RNR) under the GST. A RNR rate of 8 percent is found to be sufficient for revenue generation of the States.

9

Tax Administration under GST

9.1 GST Council

The Constitution Amendment Bill, 2014 (122nd Amendment) envisages that the administration of GST would be the responsibility of the GST Council which would then become the apex indirect tax policy making body of the country. This GST Council would be formed by the Central and State level ministers in charge of the finance portfolio. The Bill also lays down various elements of how the GST Council would operate and its powers, such as determining the rate and exemptions of tax, threshold limits, framing model laws and principles of levy and apportionment of IGST, and voting powers.

The composition of the GST Council and the voting pattern clearly spelt out that the veto power rests with the Central Government and there is a clear erosion of fiscal autonomy of the states. Given the fragile nature of the Centre-State financial relations, the introduction of GST may open a fresh bout of disputes between the Centre and the States.

9.2 Tax Administration

As under the GST, the Constitution Amendment Bill, 2014 seeks to empower both the states and the Union Government to have concurrent powers to levy GST on goods, services and imports from the production point to the final consumption and the design of dual GST proposed, the CGST and IGST would be administered by the Central Board of Excise and Customs (CBEC) and the SGST would be administered by the State Commercial Tax Departments. As the tax base is common, both the CBEC and the State Commercial Tax Departments have to deal with the same set of tax payers. All basic functions such as registration, return filing, verification of returns assessments, audit etc. may be assigned to both the Union and State tax authorities jointly so as to reduce the burden on tax administration and also to reduce compliance costs. The first and the foremost function for GST Council would be to thrash out a common threshold level for the CGST and SGST.

If the CENVAT exemption continues with the existing turnover of ₹ 1.5 crore, then the threshold limit for CGST registration will remain the same and the tax administration will have to deal with the same tax payers. Similarly, the GST Council has to build a broad consensus among the states to have a common threshold for SGST and IGST registrations.

The real challenge for the tax administration under GST will be the integration of the huge informal sector enterprises with the formal economy. Even though compliance costs are bound to increase, keeping the huge informal sector outside the tax net may be injurious to the economy in the long-run. These informal sector enterprises may be brought under the tax net through incentives. such as access to credits, providing suitable incentives for consumers to demand for invoices for all purchases made and setting up of a digital interface between the tax authorities and the consumers which would largely reduce tax evasions. The commercial banks are required to register in each state of their operation and pay the taxes separately to the State and Central Governments.

Having set the threshold levels, the tax payers are required to register on a common web portal which is to be developed exclusively (GSTN) for this purpose. In the proposed GST, there is going to be a paradigm shift in the tax administration as the Central tax authorities have to deal with the traders engaged in wholesale and retail trade apart from the existing manufacturers and the service providers. On the other hand, the state authorities would also have to deal with the manufacturers and service providers in addition to the existing traders. Therefore, the Central authorities conversant with the

CENVAT and service tax administration have to co-ordinate with the state authorities in dealing with traders and vice-versa which would be beneficial for both the tax administrations. For the benefit of tax payers, a new PAN-based tax payer ID, a common return both for SGST and CGST and a common challan for tax payment have been agreed upon.

9.3 IT Strategy for the GST

Considering the importance of IT infrastructure for GST, the Ministry of Finance with the concurrence of the Empowered Committee of State Finance Ministers had mandated the National Securities Depository Ltd. (NSDL) to develop a common portal called GST Network to carry out the functions under GST (GSTN). Regarding GST reporting, there has been a consensus among the States on a common portal which provides the basic services of registration, returns filing and payments. The pilot testing of the GSTN portal has been carried out in 11 states and found to be successful. The tax payer is required to file the returns with GSTN which in turn would send the copy of the return to the respective states and the CBEC.

Simultaneously, the tax payer has to pay the tax in a bank and the bank uploads the challans to the GSTN. This provides an opportunity to cross verify the returns with the taxes paid and avoids pilferages and fraud in tax collection. The major task for the Government would be to computerize all the states before the roll-out of the GST since information technology is going to play a vital role in providing a unified common system where the tax information can be collected centrally and distributed to all the states and the Central Government. In a similar manner, the inter-State trade on goods and services will also be brought under the IGST framework. Even though the core services viz. registration, payments and filing of returns have been brought under the common portal, the other important functions such as processing refunds, audits and appeals may also be brought under the GSTN subsequently.

9.4 Conclusion

The tax administration under GST will undergo a paradigm shift from the existing administration. The GST Council will become an important decision-making apex body to carry out the tax administration in the country. At the field level, the CBEC and State commercial tax departments have to carry out all the basic functions of the GST administration. Both the Central and State tax authorities have to deal with a new set of tax payers in addition to the existing tax payers. Hence, it becomes necessary to have tax coordination between the Central and State authorities which would be mutually beneficial. To provide a seamless network of tax operations throughout the country, an effective IT infrastructure has to be developed and put in place before the roll-out of the GST.

10

GST in Canada

10.1 Introduction

Canada is one of the federal countries offering a variety of sales tax systems in the world today. It implemented a comprehensive value added tax at the federal level covering both goods and services applicable in the entire country. It has ten provinces and five different types of sales tax systems. Alberta is one of the provinces where GST is the only tax. It draws relatively better revenues from the sale of petroleum. It does not levy provincial sales tax. In other four provinces such as British Columbia, Saskatchewan, Manitoba and Ontario, there is a separate retail sales tax (RST) system in addition to the federal GST with exclusive tax base. In the province of Prince Edward Island, the provincial RST is levied along with the federal GST. In other three provinces, namely, Newfoundland, Nova Scotia and New Brunswick, there is a joint federal-provincial VAT called harmonized sales tax (HST) administered by the federal government at a uniform rate of 15 percent. In the last province, Quebec, there is a VAT called Quebec Sales Tax (QST) in addition to the federal GST and both the taxes are administered by the provincial government.

Hence, Canada has separate federal and provincial VATs administered provincially, joint federal and provincial VATs administered federally and separate federal VAT and provincial RSTs administered separately. The above situation emerged following the decision of the federal government in 1991 replacing the age-old manufacturer's sales tax with invoice credit based destination consumption VAT. Such a decision of the federal government met with a stiff resistance from the provincial governments as most of them depended heavily on the retail sales taxes.

10.2 Federal Level GST

Goods and services tax (GST) is a comprehensive VAT at the federal level covering all the goods and services applicable from the manufacturing to the retail stage allowing input credit for all non-labour inputs excluding investment goods. Even though, it covers all goods and services, goods supplied by the governments are not covered. Dealers with a turnover of less than C$ 30,000 are also exempted. A list of select services such as residential rents, health services, education services, etc. is also exempted. Apart from this, basic essential goods such as agricultural and fish products, life saving drugs and medical devices are also zero-rated. Local governments, educational institutions and public hospitals receive partial rebate ranging from 57 percent to 83 percent on their purchases. Also, it provides credit to low income families to reduce the incidence of GST through refund cheques from the income tax department.

10.3 Provincial Sales Tax and VAT

At the provincial level, the coverage under QST and HST are comprehensive whereas RST is levied on all goods with exemptions. Hence, these provinces implementing RST covers all inputs and a few services and those with QST and HST cover services excluding investments. Basic consumer and producer goods are exempted in most of the provinces. But over the years, many services such as repairing, hotel accommodation, insurance premium, etc., were also covered. The differential RST tax rates are given in Table 10.1.

These rates are standard rates covering all commodities except special rates for alcoholic beverages which range from 8 percent to 25 percent.

10.4 Tax Administration for GST (Federal VAT)

Under the GST, dealers with a threshold level of C$ 30,000 and above are required to register their units with the tax department. The tax department assigns business numbers (BN) to the dealers after due verification of the basic information provided by the dealers. The registration of GST entails automatic registration for HST. More than 90 percent of the dealers submit their return quarterly and the remaining 10 percent monthly. For the convenience of the small traders (traders with a turnover of less than C$ 50,000, the tax department uses a quick method in which the tax liability is determined as a percentage of total sales such as vendor of goods (3 percent), vendor of services (5 percent) and grocery vendors (25 percent to 30 percent).

Table 10.1: RST Rates in Different Provinces of Canada

S. No.	Name of the Province	Tax Rate
1.	Prince Edward Island	10 percent PST
2.	Ontario	8 percent PST
3.	Manitoba	7 percent PST
4.	British Columbia	7 percent PST
5.	Saskatchewan	6 percent PST
6.	Quebec	7.5 percent VAT
7.	Newfoundland	8 percent HST (VAT)
8.	Nova Scotia	8 percent HST (VAT)
9.	New Brunswick	8 percent HST (VAT)

Auditing of dealers is one of the components of GST and the dealers are selected on a random basis based on their sector profile, financial ratios, etc. Auditing information management system provides information for verification, enforcement and compliance of dealers and such information is fed to the auditors for accomplishing their assignments. Further, management information system (MIS) provides all information regarding registration, tax payment, processing of returns and other dos and don'ts.

Bibliography

Bibliography

Bagchi, Amaresh (1994), "Reform of Domestic Trade Taxes in India: Issues and Options", National Institute of Public Finance and Policy, New Delhi.

Bagchi, Amaresh (2001), "The Way to Tax Services", *Economic Times*, April 25, 2001.

Bird, Richard M. and Gendron-Pierre-Pascal (2001), "VAT in Federal States: International Experience and Emerging Possibilities".

Burgess, R. and N. Stern (1993), "Tax Reforms in India", Working Paper No. 45, STICERD, London School of Economics.

Chelliah, Raja J. et al. (2001), "Primer on Value Added Tax", National Institute of Public Finance and Policy, New Delhi.

Chelliah, Raja J. (1991), "Tax Reforms Committee", Interim Report, Ministry of Finance, Government of India, New Delhi.

Comptroller and Auditor General of India (2010), "Implementation of VAT in India: Lessons for Transitions to GST", June.

Debonis, Valeria (1997), "Regional Integration and Commodity Tax Harmonization", The World Bank Policy Research Working Paper No. 1848.

Delipalla, Sofia (1997), "Commodity Tax Harmonization and Public Goods", *Journal of Public Economics*, Vol. 63, Elsevier, Toronto, Canada.

Edwards, Christ and Derugy (2002), "International Tax Competition", Economic Freedom of Veroniqua World 2002, Annual Report, The Fraser Institute, Vancouver, Canada.

Empowered Group on IT Infrastructure (2015), "The IT Strategy for Goods and Services Tax".

Gandelman, Neston Murillo, Hernandex Ruben (2002), "Tax Competition and Tax Harmonization with Evasion", Federal Reserve Bank of St. Louis, U.S.A.

Gordon, Jim and Poonam Gupta (2003), "Understanding India's Services Revolution", Paper prepared for the IMF-NCEAR Conference, November 14-16, New Delhi.

Government of India (1978), "Report of the Indirect Taxation Enquiry Committee", Ministry of Finance, Part II.

Government of India (1991), "Tax Reforms Committee", Ministry of

Finance Report, Part II.

Government of India (2005), "White Paper on State Level Value Added Tax", Ministry of Finance, New Delhi, January 17.

Government of India Budget (1994-95), "Speech of Shri Manmohan Singh, Minister of Finance, Presenting the Union Government's Budget for 1994-95".

Government of India, "Taxation Enquiry Commission (TEC) 1953-54", Ministry of Finance, Vol. III.

Government of India (1977), "Report of the Indirect Taxation Enquiry Committee", Part I, October, Ministry of Finance.

Government of India, Ministry of Finance, "Fiscal Responsibility and Budget Management Act, 2003".

Government of India, Ministry of Finance (2001), "Primer on Value Added Tax".

Government of India, Ministry of Finance (2002), "Task Force on Direct and Indirect Tax Reforms", Chairman: Vijay Kelkar.

Government of India, Ministry of Finance (2015), "Report on the Revenue Neutral Rate and Structure of Rates for the Goods and Services Tax (GST)", December 4, Chairman: Arvind Subramanian.

Gupta, Arindam Das (2011), "An Assessment of the Revenue Impact of the State Level VAT in India", *Economic and Political Weekly*.

Indian Tax Foundation (2003), "Tax Reforms in India: 1991-2001", New Delhi.

Joshi, V. and I.M.D. Little (1996), "India's Economic Reforms: 1991-2001", Oxford University Press, New Delhi.

Joshua, Aizeman and Yothin Jinjarak (2005), "The Collection Efficiency of the Value Added Tax: Theory and International Evidence", Working Paper No. 11539, National Bureau of Economic Research, Cambridge.

Keen, M.J. and Kostaginnasis (2004), "Tax Competition in Federations and Welfare Consequences of Decentralization", International Monetary Fund (IMF), Washington.

Keen, M.J. (2002), "Some International Issues in Commodity Taxation", *Swedish Economic Policy Review*, Vol. 9, The Economic Council of Sweden, Stockholm, Sweden.

Keen, M.J. (1987), "Welfare Effects of Commodity Tax Harmonization", *Journal of Public Economics*, Vol. 33, Elsevier, Toronto, Canada.

Keen, M.J. (1989), "Pareto-improving Indirect Tax Harmonization", *European Economic Review*, Vol. 33, Elsevier, Toronto, Canada.

Kelkar, Vijay (2003), "Task Force on Indirect Taxes", Ministry of Finance, Government of India.

Lahiri, P. and Raimondos (1998), "Public Good Provision and Welfare Effects of Indirect Tax Harmonization", *Journal of Public Economics*, Vol. 67, Elsevier, Toronto, Canada.

Lakdawala, D.T. and Nambiar, K.V. (1972), "Commodity Taxation in India", Sardar Patel Institute of Economics and Social Research, Ahmedabad.

Lockwood, Ben (1996), "Can Commodity Tax Harmonization be Pareto-improving When Government Supply Goods?", *Journal of International Economics*, Vol. 43, Elsevier, Toronto, Canada.

Lockwood, de Meza and Myles (1994), "Tax Harmonization and the Origin Principle", *Economic Letters*, Vol. 71, Elsevier, Toronto, Canada.

Mario, Alfano and Mossimo Salzano Rosario (2001), "Tax Competition in an Open Border Scenario: An Evolutionary Game and Theoretical Approach", University of Salerno, Federico Caffe Centre Research Report 1/2000, Fisciano, Italy.

McLure, C.E. (2000), "Implementing Sub-national Value Added Tax on Internal Trade and the Compensating VAT (CVAT)", *International Tax and Public Finances*, 7(6), pp. 723-740.

Mintz and Tulkens (1986), "Commodity Tax Competition between Member States of a Federation: Equilibrium and Efficiency", *Journal of Public Economics*, Vol. 29, Elsevier Toronto, Canada, pp. 133-172.

Mintz and Wilson (1991), "International VAT Monitor", International Bureau of Fiscal Documentation, Amsterdam, Vol. 7, pp. 311-323.

Mukhopadhyay, Sukumar (2002), "Excise and Customs Duty Reform", *Economic and Political Weekly*, Vol. 37, No. 4, January 26-February 1.

National Institute of Public Finance and Policy (1994), "Reform of Domestic Trade Taxes in India: Issues and Options".

Oates, W.E. (1999), "An essay on Fiscal Federalism", *Journal of Economic Literature*, Vol. 37, American Economic Association, Nashville, Tennessee, 3, September.

Poddar, Satya and Ehtisham Ahmad (2009), "GST Reforms and

Intergovernmental Considerations in India", Department of Economic Affairs, Ministry of Finance, Government of India.

Purohit, Mahesh (1975), "Sales Taxation in India: An Economic Analysis of its Structure and Operations with Special Reference to the Northern Zone", S. Chand & Co., New Delhi.

Rao, Govinda M. (2003), "Reform of Central Sales Tax in the Context of VAT", *Economic and Political Weekly*, February 15, pp. 627-636.

Rao, R. Kavita (2008), "Goods and Services Tax for India", Working Paper No. 2008-57, National Institute of Public Finance and Policy, New Delhi.

Sury, M.M. (1988), "Excise Taxation in India", Commonwealth Publishers, New Delhi, p. 42.

Virmani, Arvind (2003), "Customs Tariff Reform", Indian Council for Research on International Economic Relations, January.

Index

Index